YOUR 10 MOST SIGNIFICANT

LIFE-
DEFINING
MOMENTS

Your 10 Most Significant

LIFE-
DEFINING
MOMENTS

DAILY CHOICES

WITH THE POWER

TO TRANSFORM YOUR LIFE

JAMES EMERY WHITE

WATERBROOK
PRESS

LIFE-DEFINING MOMENTS
PUBLISHED BY WATERBROOK PRESS
2375 Telstar, Suite 160
Colorado Springs, Colorado 80920
A division of Random House, Inc.

ISBN 1-57856-454-9

Library of Congress Cataloging-in-Publication Data
White, James Emery, 1961–
    Life-defining moments : daily choices with the power to transform your life / James Emery White.—1st ed.
        p. cm.
    ISBN 1-57856-454-9
    1. Christian life. 2. Choice (Psychology)—Religious aspects—Christianity. I. Title.
BV4509.5 .W454 2001
248.4—dc21

                                                                                                    2001017946

Printed in the United States of America
2001—First Edition

10 9 8 7 6 5 4 3 2 1

CONTENTS

WORDS OF THANKS

This book was largely completed while studying at Oxford University in the summer of 2000. Thanks go to the many fine lecturers and fellow students who gave much-appreciated intellectual stimulation that stoked the fires of writing.

I am indebted to my assistant, Ms. Glynn Goble, in ways too numerous to mention. I am daily grateful for God's vocational calling on your life. As always, appreciation runs deep for the good folks of Mecklenburg Community Church, who give me the freedom and encouragement to keep writing.

This book marks a new partnership with WaterBrook Press, a division of Random House, Inc. Thanks for the vision, Erin, and for deciding to move on this project on short notice in light of an author's unique schedule. Thanks also to Ron Lee for serving as editor and believing in the project from the beginning.

As always, the greatest thanks go to my wife, Susan, who once again made every page possible. Marrying you was one of the great *kairos* moments of my life.

James Emery White
Charlotte, North Carolina

I heard in Addison's Walk a bird sing clear
"This year the summer will come true this year. This
   year.

"Winds will not strip the blossom from the apple trees
This year, nor want of rain destroy the peas.

"This year time's nature will no more defeat you,
Nor all the promised moments in their passing cheat
   you.

"This time they will not lead you round and back
To Autumn, one year older, by the well-worn track.

"This year, this year, as all these flowers foretell,
We shall escape the circle and undo the spell.

"Often deceived, yet open once again your heart,
Quick, quick, quick, quick!—the gates are drawn apart."

What the Bird Said Early in the Year

C. S. LEWIS

AN OPENING WORD

A high school English teacher took time to share her students' reactions to Kazuo Ishiguro's *The Remains of the Day*. This Booker Prize novel tells the story of Stevens, an aging butler who realizes too late that his life has been wasted through foolish choices. He must live the rest of his life without the love of the only woman he has ever cherished.

At first the students were baffled that this man's choices would have permanent consequences. They couldn't accept that despite Stevens's subsequent efforts and his strongest wishes, he must learn to live with the unhappy results of what he had done. As the classroom discussion was beginning, they asked, "Why doesn't he just act on his feelings? [Why] doesn't he just tell the housekeeper that he loves her?"

"She's married to someone else now and has a daughter," the teacher reminded them. "He can't ask her to leave her family."

"But they love each other," the students protested. All the teacher could say was, "It's too late."

"Too late" is a term that mystifies these high school students. As teenagers, they've made very few decisions that can't easily be unmade. Yet the idea is not beyond them. As graduation looms, they realize that the choices they've made about working hard or slacking off in their studies have caught up with them as scholarship offers and college acceptances appear in the mail—or don't.

A troubling thought begins to take shape in their minds. Starting now, their decisions about work and school and relationships will affect what happens tomorrow, and they ask, "What if I pick the wrong thing?"

They realize that some of their peers already have made decisions that can't be reversed. Several have babies. One is married. Many are working in after-school jobs that will become their lifetime careers. Others haven't passed the courses necessary to graduate and may never get meaningful work. All of them know students who died because someone chose to drink and drive.

Then they reflect on the adults they know, and they recognize that many are reeling from long-ago decisions that led to drug addiction and disease, soured marriages and divorces, disappointing careers and estranged offspring. Suddenly they see that the one thing they don't want is to come to the end of their lives and say, as Stevens must say in the novel, "If only I had done things differently."

The teacher doesn't want to squash her students' idealism or make them feel defeated. But she does want them to have greater respect and sympathy for those who endure rather than rage, who stay the course instead of fleeing the scene. Most important, she wants them to hold on to their hope while learning to be more cautious, more aware of the forever aspect of what they decide today.[1]

She was a very wise teacher.

Every life is defined by two movements of time, but most of us are aware only of one. We are born, we live, and we die. That is our lifetime. The Bible soberly notes that we are promised threescore years and ten, and those boundaries have yet to be moved with any great success.

There is, however, another great sweep of time that transcends the limits of hours or days. In the movie *Gladiator*, as the Roman army prepares to engage the last of the invading barbaric hordes, the Roman general Maximus cries out, "What we do now echoes in eternity."[2] And many things we do today will echo throughout eternity. Beyond the time that defines the parameters of a life, there is a time that defines the *outcome* of a life.

This reality was better understood by the ancient Greeks than by us moderns. Beyond having a word for the common passage of time, *chronos*, from which we get our word "chronological," they made use of another term, *kairos*, for which we have no counterpart in the English language. *Kairos* speaks to the quality and content of time itself, independent of its actual length. It speaks of something altogether different from chronological time. *Kairos* is time filled with opportunity, a moment pregnant with eternal significance and possibility. It is a point of time that demands action, a space of time in which life-determining decisions are made.[3] As a result, Plato wrote that anyone who misses or evades his *kairos* destroys himself: "Can there be any doubt that a work is spoilt when it is not done at the right time?"[4] *Kairos* is that decisive time, the moment that meets the challenge of shaping our destiny.

Intriguingly, the biblical writers made extensive use of this unique and provocative word. In the book of Jeremiah, Pharaoh is talked about as being a king who was only a loud noise, and nothing more, because he had missed his moment.[5] In the New Testament we find Satan leaving Jesus at the end of forty days of temptation until a more *opportune* time[6] and Jesus Himself talking about specific times of testing that await all who receive the Word of God. These times of testing, according to Jesus, will determine faith's final outcome.[7] Perhaps the most poignant reflection of this is found when Jesus came to Jerusalem. Seeing the city, He broke down in tears, because the people did not recognize the time of God's coming.[8]

Leonardo da Vinci once reflected that the average human "looks without seeing, listens without hearing, touches without feeling, eats without tasting, moves without physical awareness, inhales without awareness of odour or fragrance, and talks without thinking."[9]

He could have added, "and lives without sensing the importance of the time." In heaven's eyes, there can be little doubt about the significance that fills the *kairos* moments of life. They determine the entire trajectory of life itself. "Nothing is more critical than to recognize and respond to such a moment," writes Os Guinness. "Before will hardens into fate and choice into 'might have been,' the *[kairos]* hour is the moment when the present is at its greatest intensity and the future is uniquely open to our decision and action."[10]

We make a choice, and then the choice makes us.

In the critically acclaimed film *Dead Poets Society,* Robin Williams plays John Keating, an English teacher at an elite New England preparatory school. On the first day of the semester, he enters a classroom filled with students only to draw them away from their desks and into the hallway. There, standing in front of a large wooden case filled with the pictures and trophies of young men from years past, he looks down on his roll sheet and, searching for a name to call, addresses the class.

"Now, Mister…Pitts… Mr. Pitts, will you open your 'hymnal' to page 542. Read the first stanza of the poem."

The student finds the section and questioningly reads the title.

"'To the Virgins to Make Much of Time'?"

"Yes, that's the one." Looking at his pupils, the teacher adds, "Somewhat appropriate, isn't it?"

Knowingly the students laugh. Young Mr. Pitts begins to read the famed verse by Robert Herrick: "Gather ye rosebuds while ye may, / Old Time is still a-flying; / And this same flower that smiles today / Tomorrow will be dying."

"Thank you, Mr. Pitts. 'Gather ye rosebuds while ye may.' The Latin term for that sentiment is *'carpe diem.'* Now, who knows what that means?"

A bespectacled student near the front replies, "*'Carpe diem,'* that's 'seize the day.'"

"Very good," replies the teacher. "Mr...."

"Meeks," the student supplies.

"Meeks," repeats Keating. "'Seize the *day*.' 'Gather ye rosebuds while ye may.' Why does the writer use these lines?"

"Because he's in a hurry," offers a student.

"No!" exclaims Keating. "Ding! Thanks for playing anyway." Then, turning serious, he gives them the answer.

"Because we are food for worms, lads. Because believe it or not, each and every one of us in this room is one day going to stop breathing, turn cold, and die."

He then reveals why they are standing in the hallway.

"I would like you to step forward over here and peruse some of the faces from the past. You've walked past them many times. I don't think you've really looked at them."

The students gaze into the case full of photographs. For the first time, they look into the eyes of those who walked the hallways before them.

"They're not that different from you, are they? Same haircuts. Full of hormones, just like you. Invincible, just like you feel. The world is their oyster. They believe they're destined for great things, just like many of you. Their eyes are full of hope, just like you. Did they wait until it was too late to make from their lives even one iota of what they were capable? Because you see, gentlemen, these boys are now fertilizing daffodils. But if you listen real close, you can hear them whisper their legacy to you. Go on, lean in. Listen. You hear it?"

Then, himself whispering as if to give voice to the past,

Keating intones, "*carpe...carpe...carpe diem.* Seize the day, boys. Make your lives extraordinary."[11]

But do we know what this means? Our tendency is to think of life's defining moments in terms of personal milestones or achievements: graduating from college, getting married, having a child, landing a particular job. In truth, these are far from the most influential and eternity-filled moments that set the course of our destiny. Truly definitive moments are those that shape the deepest parts of who we are, and more important, what we are becoming. They transcend the hour of their occurrence in ways that take on lasting significance. Because of their potency, they often prove to be wildly influential not only in our own lives but in the lives of those around us.

The Bible teaches that within every life God provides such *kairos* moments and that these life-shaping doorways to the future can be identified and their opportunities seized. "Be very careful, then, how you live," wrote the apostle Paul, "not as unwise but as wise, making the most of every opportunity."[12] We must dare to exploit the *kairos* moments as they appear.

But how?

That is what our journey through this book, by God's grace, will provide. Not only will we outline ten of the most significant *kairos* moments, but we'll also explore what's involved in taking full advantage of the power of these moments in our lives. As a result, we'll not only receive each day, but we'll discern its potential. For it's within time that God meets us and draws us to the choices that will shape the contours and destiny of our lives.[13]

1

WHEN CALLED TO OBEY

"Okay, Jim, I want you to go right to the edge of the cliff, then turn around and lean out over the edge. Just do exactly what I say, and you'll be fine."

I certainly wanted to be fine, but I didn't want to do exactly what my buddy said.

We were in Colorado, and I had been talked into going mountain climbing with some now ex-friends of mine. What I didn't know was that when they said "mountain climbing," they meant actually climbing up mountains. No little hills or picturesque paths with a gradual upward slant. We were scaling the face of a cliff, going from ledge to ledge, foothold to foothold.

Now here's where I reveal the depth of my intellect. I don't know why, but the whole time we were inching our way to the top, it never entered my mind how we were going to get down. I guess I assumed we'd walk down a trail on the backside of the mountain.

But no.

After we reached the summit, I saw that there was no gently

sloping backside. Instead there was a sheer drop-off on all sides. Suddenly the matter of how we were going to get back down entered my mind. Turning to the men in my group, with something of a nervous laugh, I said, "Uh, guys, just how are we going to get down from here?"

Their answer will forever echo in my mind. "We rappel."

As far as I knew, rappelling had little to do with God or the things of God. Rappelling involves hooking yourself up to a rope, edging out to the top of a precipice, leaning out at a ninety-degree angle, and then shuffling your way down the face of the cliff. A thin nylon rope is all that stands between you and plummeting to a certain death. Now you know why these guys are my ex-friends.

I had options. I could have stayed forever on the mountain. I could have waved down a passing helicopter. Neither of those approaches was particularly viable. So for the next twenty minutes, I did everything I was told without question. It was frightening and it went completely against my better judgment. I had to place a counterintuitive trust in someone other than me. I went against every natural impulse within me, and I succeeded. I'm off the top of that mountain, which has had a rather distinctive impact on the rest of my life.

There are times when choosing to obey determines everything that comes afterward. It's a *kairos* moment that bears significance far beyond the decision itself. In the book of Numbers, the Bible tells of a time when the people of Israel were moving across a desert and had no water to drink. Moses and his brother, Aaron, sought the counsel of God at the entrance to the Tent of Meeting, and the glory of God appeared to them. The voice of the Lord said to Moses, "Take the staff, and you and your brother Aaron gather the assembly together. Speak to that rock before their eyes and it will pour out its water."[1]

Moses didn't do it though. When he gathered the people together, instead of speaking to the rock as God had prescribed, he chose to go his own way. He struck the rock with his staff. Twice.

It would seem to be a minor variation on a theme. But it was much more than that. Moses knowingly, willfully disobeyed the Lord. He knew God's directive, but he chose not to follow it. He didn't trust God enough to believe that what He had prescribed was best. Intriguingly, water still came forth from the rock. The consequences of disobedience aren't always immediate. But soon thereafter, God told Moses, "Because you did not trust in me…you will not bring this community into the land I give them."[2] A solitary act of disobedience dramatically shaped the remaining course of Moses' life. When we are faced with the choice to obey or disregard the commands of the living God, we enter into a moment that is filled with lasting consequence.

Think of obedience to God as coming to a fork in the road. You can go right or left. Taking the way of God keeps you securely in His perfect will. When you choose a path of disobedience, however, your steps take you away from God's perfect desires. Nothing less than a new trail has been blazed, and that trail directs you to unavoidable outcomes. Or as Robert Frost reflected on the various paths we take, "way leads on to way."[3]

Life is full of such *kairos* moments. Some forks in the road present us with greater consequences than others. And at each juncture, with every divergence, we can continue to move away from the life God intended for us or we can maneuver back toward it. But make no mistake: Such choices are like stones thrown into a pool of standing water. They cause ripples throughout the remainder of our lives.

This idea of one brief moment having lifelong consequences is a difficult one to entertain. We shy away from it. Instead of gazing farther down our chosen path to look at its inevitable implications, we prefer to look around for an escape route. When we've wandered into the desert of disobedience, we want to drink deeply from the well of forgiveness and have that eliminate all consequences.

But it doesn't.

Moses no doubt regretted his disobedient action, and God is faithful to forgive anyone who has a repentant heart. But the Lord's forgiveness doesn't diminish the repercussions of a decision to disobey. The clock can't be turned back. So it was Joshua, not Moses, who led the people of Israel across the Jordan River. Moses was allowed to look across the river into the Promised Land. But his earlier decision to disobey prevented him from crossing over with the people.[4]

What if Moses had obeyed God's command to speak to the rock rather than choosing to strike it? What could his life have been like? We don't know any more than we know what our lives would be like if we were free of the vast array of disobedient choices we've made. The wrong choices have been made, and they impact our lives far more than we can imagine.

In order to seize the day in regard to obedience, we must become aware of what drives us to disobedience. The apostle Paul admitted, "For what I do is not the good I want to do; no, the evil I do not want to do—this I keep on doing."[5] This tension between wanting to do right but failing to do so is the great dynamic of our lives. Knowing why is the first step toward wresting our destiny back from its grip.

Why We Disobey

If you have the chance to interact with children on a regular basis, you know that some kids are naturally compliant, but many—in fact, most—aren't. My older daughter, Rebecca, was one of those rare children who was more than willing to comply with every request. Except for the "times."

During her threes and fours, there were half a dozen instances when Rebecca suddenly abandoned her agreeable nature and steadfastly refused to do whatever it was that we'd asked her to do. In our routine of saying, "Rebecca, pick up your toy and put it back into the box" or "Rebecca, tell your sister that you're sorry," there were sudden intrusions when one of our standard requests would be met with an icy silence, a standing of her ground, a pursing of her lips, and a resolute look in her eyes. And then we knew. It was going to be one of those "times."

They were long, drawn out, defiant; truly a battle of wills. She simply wasn't going to do what we told her to do. At least not without a fight.

What causes disobedience? The theological answer is hardly a mystery: Sin has marred our ability to follow the perfect will of God. The heart of God's desire for us is thwarted by the independent exercise of our free will. Since the time of Adam, we've used our will to act independently of God's leadership. We've wanted to be our own god.

True enough. But what are we thinking?

Ask a man who hasn't yet engaged in an illicit affair if he believes pursuing such a course of action would be wise, much less moral, and he'll say, "Of course not." Then six months later you watch as he rushes headlong into an adulterous relationship. What is he thinking?

Ask anyone you talk to if it's best to lie, and he or she will say, "Certainly not." Later, though, when backed into an awkward corner on a particular issue, a person's tongue quickly begins to spread deceit.

What is it that takes hold and drives us to choices that contradict our stated beliefs? Why do we take paths that will mar the complexion of our lives? Consider the following six dynamics, which begin to explain why we do things we know aren't the best for us.

Ignorance

I once read about a sweet old lady who was a bit conservative in her mannerisms and behavior. She wanted to plan a week's vacation at a Florida campground, so she wrote a letter to the manager to find out about availability and services.

Foremost in her mind was whether the campground had a toilet. But she couldn't bring herself to write the word "toilet" in a letter. She considered writing "bathroom commode." But even that was tough for her to put down on paper. So she decided to use an abbreviation, asking in her letter if the campground had its own "BC."

When the campground owner received the letter, he was baffled. He didn't have any idea what "BC" referred to. He decided it had to refer to a local Baptist church. So this is what he wrote back to his elderly correspondent:

Dear Madam:

I am pleased to inform you that a BC is located nine miles north of the campground, and is capable of seating 250 people at one time. I admit it is quite a distance away if you are in the habit of going regularly, but no doubt you will be pleased to know that a great number of people take their lunches along and make a day of it.

The last time my wife and I went was six years ago, and it was so crowded we had to stand up the whole time we were there.

I would like to say that it pains me very much not to be able to go more regularly, but it surely is no lack of desire on my part. As we grow older, it seems to be more of an effort, particularly in cold weather.

If you decide to come down to our campground, perhaps I could go with you the first time, sit with you, and introduce you to all the other folks. This is a friendly community.[6]

We smile, but it's amazing how easy it is to be unaware of what is really being asked of us. One of the biggest reasons people disobey—particularly if they are relatively new or unschooled in their faith—is that they don't know what it is that God would have them do. Much like Paul's interaction with a group of well-intentioned folk who wanted to be followers of Christ but who never had heard of the Holy Spirit. In fact, they'd never been told there was anything beyond the baptism of John the Baptist.[7] You can't obey what you don't know to obey, and I've worked with too many young believers to underestimate the degree of spiritual illiteracy that can be brought to the table of faith.

But the same thing is true of anyone's introduction to something new. If you're a golfer, you've probably read, or at last heard about, the popular little red book. That's the title: *Harvey Penick's Little Red Book*. Back in the 1920s, Harvey Penick bought a red spiral notebook and began jotting down observations about golf. He never showed it to anyone except his son until 1991, when he shared it with a writer and asked if it might be worth publishing. The man told Penick he thought he ought to give it a try. In fact, the writer contacted Simon & Schuster, where an editor loved the idea and offered an advance of ninety thousand dollars. The writer called and left word with Penick's wife about the money and the proposed book deal.

When the writer saw Penick later, the old man seemed troubled, even a bit sad. His friend asked what was wrong, and Penick told him that with all of his medical bills there was no way he could pay the publisher that much money. He had no idea that it was Simon & Schuster that would advance the ninety thousand dollars to *him!* He knew so little about the publishing business that he thought he'd have to pay to have his book published.

But he learned fast. *Harvey Penick's Little Red Book* has sold more than a million copies, making it one of the most successful sports books ever published.[8]

Penick's ignorance of the rules of publishing could have prevented him from getting his book in the hands of millions of golf lovers, and it could have meant the loss of tens of thousands of dollars. But he learned the rules and acted accordingly. We can do the same to overcome our ignorance of what God wants from us.

Rebellion

The exact opposite of ignorance is rebellion. When ignorance leads to disobedience, it's not willful in nature. But rebellion is purposeful in its rejection of authority. As people with a sinful disposition, we already are oriented toward all forms of rebellion. It doesn't matter what the issue is, we tend to resist the idea of submitting to another authority. It chafes against our souls.

Rather than submit, we boldly pursue the momentary pleasure of indulging our fleshly desires. We recognize the conflict between what we want and what God asks of us, and we defiantly choose our own way. There is a current running within all of us that shouts, "Don't tell me what to do!" While this tendency is universal, it betrays an absence of intimacy in our relationship with Christ. It was Jesus Himself Who said, "If anyone loves me, he will obey my teaching.… He who does not love me will not obey my teaching."[9] Far from being a dead, lifeless list of dos and don'ts, obedience is a matter of the heart, flowing from a relationship. It's not an "ought to" as much as a "want to." It's not duty as much as devotion.

Fear

My grandmother was terrified of storms. If her fear of the weather didn't border on the phobic, it was at the very least flamingly neurotic. My mother recalls being forced as a young girl to huddle around a car tire in the living room with her brother, all feet against the rubber, as protection against a lightning strike. If a cloud appeared on the horizon, Mama Keele would race home, turn on the television for the weather report, and fret away the hours. Once, while joining us on a family beach trip about twenty miles from her house, my grandmother spotted a cloud. She immediately demanded to be taken home, insisting that we all accompany her. My parents tried to calm her fears, but her anxiety only grew. She announced that if we didn't leave that instant, she'd just walk home. Assessing the situation at the ripe old age of three, I offered to walk with her.

My grandmother always loved me for that.

Many times fear lies behind our choice to disobey. Think of the times we tell a lie. More often than not, we believe a lie will produce better results than telling the truth. Ironically, we opt for the untruth because we fear the consequences of obedience. We're like the rich young ruler who walked away rather than act on Jesus' demands to abandon his materialistic lifestyle. We believe that what we'd lose in following Christ is too great a cost. We value what we already have more than the riches we would gain in obeying Him.

I read about a spy who was captured and then sentenced to death by a general who had the strange custom of giving condemned criminals a choice between a firing squad and a big, black door. As the moment of execution drew near, the spy was brought to the general, who asked, "What will it be: the firing squad or the door?"

The spy hesitated, but in the end he chose the firing squad. The shots rang out, and he slumped over dead.

The general turned to his aide and said, "They always prefer the known to the unknown. But he had a choice."

The aide then asked, "Sir, what is behind the door?"

"Freedom," the general replied. "But only a few have been brave enough to take it."[10]

Letting go of what we know in order to lay hold of the wealth that comes with obedience strikes fear in our hearts. The comfort we find in the familiar terrain of the present keeps us from taking the risky step of obedience, which leads us into a much more desirable future. There can be little doubt that acting in obedience to Christ calls us to act against our deepest fears.

Rationalization

A third dynamic that often underlies our disobedience is simple rationalization. We convince ourselves that our course of action is not wrong—at least for us. We feel there is some "cosmic exception clause" written into our spiritual contract. We acknowledge what God has said about the matter we are facing, but we believe our particular circumstance calls for the exercise of the exception clause. Such disobedience, we reason, is not truly disobedience at all.

The Bible anticipates this mind-set and speaks to it with great clarity. "The man who says, 'I know him,' but does not do what he commands is a liar, and the truth is not in him. But if anyone obeys his word, God's love is truly made complete in him. This is how we know we are in him: Whoever claims to live in him must walk as Jesus did."[11] "Only he who believes is obedient," noted Dietrich Bonhoeffer, and "only he who is obedient believes."[12]

Rationalization and true life in Christ can't coexist. The one will cancel out the other. If we truly love and trust Christ, we will obey Him. If we reason our way out of obeying Him, then the life we claim to live in Him ceases to have integrity. We can't have it both ways.

Selectivity

Another force behind our disobedience is selectivity, a kind of "salad bar" approach to God's directives. You grab your tray and start down the line. If you notice a biblical directive that will help out your marriage or your parenting responsibilities, you gladly follow its prescription. But if you run into something you don't like—something that would require life-changing and disruptive obedience—you simply pass it by. It's easier to disregard the less-appealing commands since you do, in fact, have some food on your plate. You can tell yourself that you're being obedient in a general sense, which seems to cover those other occasions of disregarding God's more stringent demands.

But selective obedience is partial obedience, which is not obedience at all.

When dedicating the Free University of Amsterdam, Dutch reformer Abraham Kuyper declared that there is not one square inch of our lives that Christ does not claim as His own. His point was valid but not entirely original. Speaking of selective obedience two thousand years ago, Christ declared: "Not all who sound religious are really godly people. They may refer to me as 'Lord,' but still won't get to heaven. For the decisive question is whether they obey my Father in heaven. At the Judgment many will tell me, 'Lord, Lord.'... But I will reply, 'You have never been mine. Go away.'"[13]

While a life completely free of disobedience is impossible this side of heaven, an authentic relationship with Christ can't be separated from a heart that is bent toward obedience. Perfect behavior is not the measure, since our words and actions always will fall short. But a heart that is sold-out to obeying God can't be faked. Jesus alone knows our hearts.

Minimalizing

There's one more reason we often choose to disobey. We know we're doing wrong, but we downplay the severity of sin. Speaking of the people of his day, the prophet Jeremiah proclaimed: "Are they ashamed of their loathsome conduct? No, they have no shame at all; they do not even know how to blush."[14] This absence of shame doesn't apply only to the Hebrews of the Old Testament. Any of us can develop a callousness that frees us to pursue the wrong course of action, and to do so without great concern. This often is coupled with a presumption upon grace that says, "I know it's wrong, and I know that I'll have to ask God to forgive me, but I'll deal with that later." We will, in fact, deal with it later. But do we realize what a truly frightening statement this is?

Minimizing the seriousness of our disobedience is a short-sighted attempt to deal with our tendency to sin. But it does nothing to minimize the mark that disobedience leaves on our lives. Yes, there is forgiveness. But there is no escaping the lasting effects of our failure to obey.

No matter what motivates our wrong choices, the inevitable truth is that disobedience brings a distortion to life. The Bible reminds us that "God's laws are perfect. They protect us, make us wise, and give us joy and light.... For they warn us away from harm and give success to those who obey them."[15] There's a good reason for these statements. Since God made us, He is the only one Who knows the optimum way for us to operate. There's no one with more insight, more knowledge, more understanding, or more wisdom.

But our motivation in obeying God isn't simply because it will lead to "the good life." People often live in obedience to the Lord and still face a life of trials, loss, and grief. God doesn't guarantee our personal comfort or our financial prosperity. Ultimately, the goal of obedience is the prostrating of one's life before the Lord of the universe. It's the yielding of a soul to its Maker. This is why authentic obedience transcends mere rules of morality. Because choices related to obedience are *kairos* moments, these moments can either transform us into the radiant image of God or the shadowed visage of the evil one.

CREATING A LIFE OF OBEDIENCE

If daily submission to God is really that important, how can we redirect our natural tendencies toward rebellion to an ingrained habit of obedience? When the *kairos* moments present themselves, how can we choose to walk according to God's way? When approaching a fork in the road and deciding on which course to follow, consider these four steps before proceeding.

Get Directions
My wife tells me that when I drive, I don't like anyone else who's on the road. With great sensitivity and compassion, I tell her it's

because most people drive like they've undergone a full frontal lobotomy. I also believe there's a secret organization whose only job is to dispatch an entire squad of irritating drivers the moment I pull out of my driveway. These innocent-looking motorists take their job seriously, and they're remarkably successful. I really do get irritated. If only my wife could see where the true fault lies.

But she's too busy observing another of my driving habits. She says I won't ever admit that I don't know where we're going. That's simply not true. I may not know exactly where I am, but I always know where I'm *going.* There's a big difference.

My male readers understand this, but my wife can get feisty about it. The other day she asked me if I knew why it takes one million sperm to fertilize a single female egg.

"No," I answered, "why?"

"Because," she deadpanned, "none of them will ever stop and ask for directions."

I still fail to find the humor in that joke. But even for us guys, the first step toward obedience is stopping to get directions, and those directions are found in the Bible.

I once listened to an interview of a well-known author who had just released his latest book. He answered the usual questions about why he wrote it, how he wrote it, and what he hoped would be the impact on people when they read it. Then he was peppered with questions on the book's content. The interviewer wanted him to tell everyone what it *said.*

"Well, read the book," the author responded. "That's why I wrote it."

But the questions continued. Finally the author said, "Listen, the whole reason I wrote the book was to answer those questions. If I wanted to answer them in a press conference, I wouldn't have written the book. So please, if you're interested in the answer, read the book! There's really no substitute."

Sometimes I wonder if God would like to stand in the middle of life's intersections, His hands upraised, stopping the traffic of humanity to tell us: "Just read the Book! That's why I wrote it!" When it comes to obedience, the writer of Psalm 119 revealed one of the great secrets of life: "Your word is a lamp to my feet and a light for my path."[16]

The directions are there. All we have to do is read them.

Talk to God

When seeking the path of obedience, a second essential consideration is whether we have talked to God about the matter. The Bible is very clear on this when it says, "If any of you lacks wisdom, he should ask God, who gives generously to all without finding fault, and it will be given to him."[17]

One of the things prayer will do is open you up to God's promptings through the Holy Spirit. The Bible speaks of God's guiding voice that comes to us when we quiet ourselves before Him. Call it a leading, call it an inner sense, call it an awareness, but it is real and unmistakable.

There is a caveat. You must judge these inner promptings by the revealed Word of God. The Holy Spirit will never direct you toward anything that contradicts the Scriptures. That would make Him confused or, even worse, deceptive. The Holy Spirit is neither.

Prayer also invites the power and presence of God into your decision about which path to follow. Obedience is not natural. It's *super*natural. You'll need the power of the Holy Spirit coursing through you in order to form your will into a shape that doesn't come automatically.

Seek Out Counsel

When we're serious about obeying God, we'll gladly take advantage of a third resource: godly counsel. In straight talk, it's the difference between laying hold of wisdom or being a fool.[18] When a person is walking down the path of disobedience, he often surrounds himself with those who tell him what he wants to hear, while cutting himself off from those who would confront him with uncomfortable challenges.

Living obediently doesn't mean you run your life by committee or that you must instantly assume that if someone tells you something that differs from what you feel is right, that you are automatically wrong. Seeking counsel is simply benefiting from the wisdom, experience, maturity, and knowledge of others who are in a vibrant, obedient relationship with Christ. You do yourself a disservice if you fail to take advantage of this invaluable resource.

Trust

The fourth step to a life of obedience is trust. After searching the Scriptures, praying, listening to the Holy Spirit, and seeking godly counsel, you'll probably have a pretty clear sense of true north. Now comes the critical moment—will you trust the course you have been shown?

In the final installment of the Indiana Jones film trilogy, Harrison Ford seeks to find the Holy Grail, the fount of eternal youth. When it is discovered, the hero is confronted with a series of trials. He can't claim the long-sought-after prize without first overcoming the obstacles, including a huge chasm that can be crossed only by a "step of faith." No path is visible, no bridge is in sight. The only option is a step into the unknown. So Indiana Jones shuts his eyes and places a foot forward into the abyss, only to discover solid ground that was invisible from the precipice.

Likewise, the promise of God to His obedient followers is solid ground, even when it's not clearly in view. The Bible tells us that "[a]nyone who trusts in him [God] will never be disappointed."[19] The relationship between trust and obedience can't be disregarded. You must settle within yourself whether God can be trusted, because without trust in Him—His Person, His character, His love—you won't obey. This is true particularly if the act of obedience initially brings sacrifice, suffering, or hardship.

A MIDCOURSE CORRECTION

If you realize you've been following a course of disobedience, stop, get your bearings, and take steps to get back on track. One of the great tragedies in life is to make a mistake, or a series of mistakes, and then feel that all is lost. Mistakes are inevitable, but our missteps don't affect God's ability to rescue us.

C. S. Lewis wrote that the "road to Hell" often is "the gradual one—the gentle slope, soft underfoot, without sudden turnings, without milestones, without signposts."[20] You may have taken a left turn when you should have stayed in the right-turn-only lane. But rather than give in to a life of fatalistic resignation, approach the next fork in the road as a *kairos* moment. It's a moment of decisive action that will mark the rest of your life.

God is still strong to save those who have strayed. He invites you to continue your journey by getting back on His path.

2

WHEN SEEKING TO BE KNOWN

The father wanted to teach his six-year-old daughter about the harsh realities of life. He stood her on the edge of her bed then backed away a couple of feet and said, "Jump, honey, I'll catch you!"

Hesitantly the little girl leaped off the bed, expecting to be caught. But her father moved back and let her fall to the floor. When she hit the ground, she cried, "Why did you drop me, Daddy?"

"Because," her father answered, "I want you to learn not to trust anyone."[1]

Few of us have experienced such cruelty at the hands of a parent. Most of us, however, know how this little girl felt. We've leaped into the arms of others only to hit the ground with a life-shattering crash. We've been abandoned, taken advantage of, betrayed, and misunderstood. We all have been deeply wounded by others. And as a result, we've learned not to trust.

We harden ourselves, lock up our hearts, and throw away the

key. Nobody gets in, for when they do, it only means pain. We drift through life emotionally detached from others. We don't allow people to get too close. While in one sense this keeps us from being hurt, it actually leads to a different type of hurt. If there is any pain worse than being wounded through a relationship, it's shutting ourselves off from relationships and enduring the suffering that comes from isolation and loneliness.

Confession time. I grew up convinced that it was never wise to tell anyone anything personal about me, because they would only use it against me later. I decided I wouldn't open up, and I wouldn't trust others. People and relationships meant betrayal, rejection, and disappointment. As a result, I became fiercely independent. It just seemed the safe way to live. And it still does.

Now it's your turn.

- Is it difficult for you to open up about your real feelings and problems?
- Is it hard for you to see other people as a source of emotional and spiritual support?
- Do you prefer to be left alone to deal with your problems?
- Are intimate, vulnerable, two-way conversations with others more of a rarity than a regular event?
- Do you find most of your personal connections revolving more around activities than relationships?[2]

If you answered yes more than a time or two, there is an important journey we both must take. Knowing and being known are not simply nice concepts. They constitute a *kairos* moment that will shape who we are and who we can become throughout the course of our lives. Knowing and being known make up the essence of the life God intended for us from the dawn of creation. As author Anne Lamott reflects in the chronicle of her own spiritual journey, "Most of the people I know who have what I want—which is to say, purpose, heart, balance, gratitude, joy—are people…in community."[3] There's a good reason for that. We were created to know others and to be known by others. And that happens in community.

The doctrine of the Trinity teaches that God is three persons yet one God. We believe in God the Father, God the Son, and God the Holy Spirit. God created a people to live in community with Him and with one another. The early Christian mystic Meister Eckhart believed we were created out of the laughter of the Trinity.[4]

"Think of your best moments of love or friendship or creative partnership, the best times with family or friends around the dinner table, your richest conversations, the acts of simple kindness that sometimes seem like the only things that make life worth living," wrote Brent Curtis and John Eldredge. "Like the shimmer of sunlight on a lake, these are reflections of the love that flows among the Trinity. We long for intimacy because we are made in the image of perfect intimacy."[5]

One of the most profound passages in the Bible is found in the second chapter of Genesis. God had created Adam, but then look at what He said about His creation: "It is not good for the man to be alone. I will make a companion who will help him."[6] That's a verse we frequently pull out at weddings, but it's much deeper than a simple message about Adam needing a helper. God was making a declaration about the importance of relationships. We need intimacy with others. The lie is that we can do life on our own, or even worse, that it's best to negotiate the joys and difficulties of life alone. The truth is very, very different. When we don't open ourselves up to others, relating beyond a superficial level, we become emotionally and spiritually dysfunctional—even to the point of physical death.

During World War II, doctors identified a fatal and mysterious illness they called marasmus. It was discovered in a group of orphaned babies who'd been placed in a care facility with brightly colored toys, new furniture, and good food. Yet the health of the children rapidly deteriorated. Over time, the babies ignored the toys and left their food largely untouched. Their systems weakened; they became lethargic. Some of the children died.

Doctors from the United Nations were flown in to attempt a diagnosis and offer treatment. After a brief investigation, they made a simple prescription that cured the problem in a matter of days: For ten minutes each hour, the children were to be picked up by a nurse, hugged, kissed, played with, and talked to. Their marasmus was cured.[7] All they needed was relational bonding.

The spiritual consequences of isolation are equally compelling. The hidden, closed life shuts us off from the community we've been called to enter as followers of Christ. It also robs us of the role that community was designed to bring to the formation of our souls. A study was performed on what differentiated Christian leaders who completed their careers with their integrity and reputations intact from those who wound up in some type of moral ditch. Of the many characteristics that emerged, one stood supreme. Those who ran their life's course to the end without stumbling had maintained significant, intimate relationships with others to whom they were truly known.[8]

Dietrich Bonhoeffer became aware of this through his own experiences with Christian community, concluding that "[t]he more isolated a person is, the more destructive will be the power of sin over him, and the more deeply he becomes involved in it, the more disastrous is his isolation."[9]

There can be little doubt that apart from community, we are emotionally and spiritually vulnerable. Church historian Martin Marty goes so far as to declare, "We have friends, or we are friends, in order that we do not get killed."[10] Yet when psychologist Larry Crabb conducted an informal survey, asking Christians if they had someone in their lives whose strength and wisdom encouraged them to make themselves fully known, the answer was uniform: "I'd give my right arm to have someone like that in my life. There's so much going on inside me that I'd love to share, not to find answers necessarily but just so someone knew. But I have no one like that."[11]

So how can we seize the moment when the opportunity for intimacy presents itself? How can we follow the Bible's admonition to "open your hearts to one another as Christ has opened his heart to you"?[12] It begins with understanding something of the dynamics of relational life.

THE LEVELS OF RELATIONSHIPS

There are at least three levels of relationships, with varying degrees of intimacy, available to us. Speaking of these levels is simplistic and risks overgeneralization, I know, but painting the canvas of relationships with such broad strokes can actually help us gain some key insights.

Acquaintance. The first, and least intimate, level is that of acquaintance. When it comes to knowing and being known, this is the most superficial. The other person might be a colleague or an associate in another department at work, or he might be a neighbor with whom you interact only on occasion. Yes, you know him, even speak to him, but you aren't intimate. You may not even like the person.

Friend. The second, more intimate, level is that of friend. Two things distinguish a friend from an acquaintance: knowledge and experience. We know things about a friend that we don't know about others. That's because a friend reveals something of who she is to us, and we layer that knowledge over a set of experiences that build common ground.

Intimate friend. While getting to know a friend is good, it can be, and often is, a very superficial relationship. There is a third level of relational intimacy that is the most meaningful of all—that of intimate friend. The key word here is *intimate.* As the apostle Paul reminded the Christians at Thessalonica: "We loved you so much that we were delighted to share with you not only the gospel of

God but our lives as well."[13] The word Paul used for "lives" was the Greek word for soul, the inner world.

The Bible describes the relationship of intimate friend in many ways, not the least of which is through a series of verses known as the "one-anothers." Found throughout Scripture, these passages provide a challenging picture of relational intimacy. For example, Jesus said, "A new command I give you: Love one another. As I have loved you, so you must love one another."[14] Relational intimacy rests on the care, concern, kindness, and acceptance that flows from the love between two people.

Consider this surgeon's observation of just such love:

I stand by the bed where a young woman lies, her face post-operative, her mouth twisted in palsy, clownish. A tiny twig of the facial nerve, the one to the muscles of her mouth, has been severed. She will be thus from now on...to remove the tumor in her cheek, I had to cut the little nerve.

Her young husband is in the room. He stands on the opposite side of the bed.... The young woman speaks.

"Will my mouth always be like this?" she asks.

"Yes," I say, "it will. It is because the nerve was cut."

She nods, and is silent. But the young man smiles.

"I like it," he says. "It is kind of cute."

...Unmindful, he bends to kiss her crooked mouth, and I so close I can see how he twists his lips to accommodate to hers, to show her that their kiss still works.... I hold my breath and let the wonder in.[15]

This young husband demonstrated what it means to love one another.

A second insight into "one another" intimacy is found in the New Testament book of Colossians, where the Bible says to "bear with each other and forgive whatever grievances you may have against one another. Forgive as the Lord forgave you."[16] To "bear with" someone means we put up with him in spite of all the difficulties involved in doing so. To be in a forgiving relationship with someone means to keep the slate clean, to continually forget the wrongs the person has done against us.

A third picture of "one another" intimacy is this: "encourage one another and build each other up."[17] The word *encourage* means to "put courage in." It is the opposite of tearing someone down. An intimate relationship strengthens us to be the people we want to be, with the kind of character and commitment that honors God. Related to this is a verse that says, "[L]et us consider how we may spur one another on toward love and good deeds.... [L]et us encourage one another."[18] To "consider" how to do something for someone else means we intentionally give it thought. Within intimacy, one friend sits down and asks herself, "How can I help this person I care about become all that God wants her to be?"

A physician was visiting one of London's leading hospitals. He entered a convalescent ward full of children whose illnesses required a long recovery period. All of the young patients were gathered at one end of the room, dressing their dolls or playing games. All the children, that is, except one little girl.

She sat by herself, alone on the edge of a high, narrow bed, holding a cheap little doll. The doctor took one look at her then turned to the head nurse and asked why the little girl was by herself.

"Her name is Susan," the nurse offered, "and we've tried to get her to play, but the other children won't have anything to do with her."

"Why not?" the doctor pressed.

"Because no one comes to see her," the nurse explained. "Her mother is dead, and her father has been here just once. When he came, he brought that little doll. The children have a strange code. Visitors mean everything. If you don't have anyone come to see you, then you aren't seen as very important or of much worth. Since no one has ever visited Susan, the other children have ignored and rejected her."

The physician immediately walked over to Susan's bed, and in a voice loud enough for the other children to hear, he said, "May I sit down, please?"

The little girl's eyes lit up.

The doctor sat down and again, loud enough for everyone to hear, said, "I can't stay very long this visit, but I have wanted to see you so badly." He asked about the health of her doll and solemnly pulled out his stethoscope to listen to the little doll's heartbeat. As he left, he turned to Susan and again, loud enough for every-one to hear, said, "You won't forget our little secret, will you? And remember, don't tell anyone!" When he got to the door, he looked back. All the other children were gathered around Susan.

Someone had finally "considered" this little girl. One can only imagine how the concern shown by a kind doctor changed her life.[19]

A final "one-another" command merits our attention. Found within the nuts-and-bolts writing of James, it says, "confess your sins to each other and pray for each other."[20]

You say, "Wow, that *is* intimate." Yes it is, but it's also integral to the depth and power God wants to bring to our lives through intimate community with others. Inherent within this is not simply opening yourself up for confession, but also admonishment. Paul's New Testament letter to Titus speaks to the importance of this, tying it to the state of being "sound in the faith."[21]

My friend Paul described how one of his intimate friends did this for him. His son was playing in a key basketball game for his high school. Paul was called out of town to address a major problem within the organization he helped lead. He didn't *have* to go, but his presence would be invaluable, and it was an important issue. He talked it over with his son, who was quick to say that he understood, so Paul felt the freedom to go.

Paul's friend went to the game in his stead, where he had the joy of seeing the son not only play but make the game-winning basket. Later, as the friend was telling Paul about the game, Paul asked if the friend thought he'd been wrong to take the business trip.

"I think you should have been at the game," his friend said

honestly. "And it's not just this game. You're traveling too much. Paul, I think you're blowing it with your son."

That night Paul asked his son about the game. Then he brought up his travel schedule, and for the first time his son was honest about how he really felt. He told his father how much it hurt him that he wasn't there. From that, Paul made changes in his life. A family became knit together, and a son bonded with his father.

Paul's honest talk with an intimate friend was a *kairos* experience, a single moment filled with lasting significance. But it wouldn't have happened apart from knowing and being known.

STEPS TOWARD INTIMACY

With a picture of what community with others can and should hold, the issue then becomes "how." This is no small issue. As John Powell writes, "I am afraid to tell you who I am, because if I tell you who I am, you may not like who I am, and it's all that I have."[22] People with a casual flippancy about moving into deep levels of relational openness are either unconscionable extroverts or have never been wounded. The rest of us think in terms of steps— each one small, reasoned, and carefully chosen—that gradually will bring us into intimacy with others without violating our already-fragile emotions.

Step 1: Admit the need. We won't make the effort to form intimate friendships if we don't first admit that we need that type of relationship. This must go beyond admitting the mere *desire* for a close relationship; we must admit that we have a deep *need* to be in community with others. And in admitting this need, we aren't becoming weak or soft. The Scriptures tell us: "Two are better than one, because they have a good return for their work: If one falls down, his friend can help him up. But pity the man who falls and has no one to help him up!"[23]

Step 2: Take the initiative. Relationships won't just happen; we have to decide we want them and then seek them out. I'm continually amazed at how many people think relationships will simply walk into their lives. To know and be known demands making the effort to know and be known. Even in the best of settings, the most friendly of environments, or the most open of communities, a move toward another person is critical.

Step 3: Take the risk. The biggest roadblock to forming deep relationships is fear. We don't take the necessary risks because we fear the outcome—rejection, misunderstandings, hurt feelings. Because some relationships in the past have gone sour, we fear we'll be wounded if we open up again. Intimacy creates a frightening level of vulnerability. Knowledge is, in a sense, power. When we allow others to get to know us, we give them the power to accept or reject us, to protect or exploit us, and that is a force that terrifies us.

And well it should.

When my older son, Jonathan, was five, I told him that he couldn't go to a particular playground near our house unless I went with him. He wanted to know why. I told him it was because it wasn't safe. He wanted to know why it wasn't safe. I told him it was because there might be a lot of strangers around, and I wanted to be careful about his safety. He wanted to know why I had to be so careful.

I was getting tired of my son's whys, and I faced the huge temptation to pull out every parent's ultimate conversation-ender by yelling, "*Because I said so!*" But I knew that wouldn't be the most patient response, so I simply *said*, "Because I said so." Actually I knew this conversation was unavoidable, so we started to talk about the differences between safe people and not-so-safe people. I think I got through to him (you never know when they're five). But I only told him half the story. While we talked about issues related to physical safety, I knew there would come a time when we'd need to talk about emotional safety. And that talk would prove to be the most difficult of all.

A safe person is someone who is just that—safe. He can be trusted. She is accepting and supportive. A safe person lets us love and be loved. We all want and need safe people in our lives. The risk is that we'll open ourselves up to someone who isn't safe. The stakes are high: Unsafe people abandon others, take advantage, betray, misunderstand, and even attack.

The *kairos* nature of this moment demands that we take a gamble, but that's not the same as reckless abandon. We need to use discernment when deciding to entrust ourselves to others. The psalmist maintained that "[i]t is better to take refuge in the LORD than to trust in man,"[24] and in the same regard, Jesus Himself was well aware of the risks involved.

During the time he was in Jerusalem, those days of the Passover Feast, many people noticed the signs he was displaying and, seeing they pointed straight to God, entrusted their lives to him. But Jesus didn't entrust his life to them. He knew them inside and out, knew how untrustworthy they were. He didn't need any help in seeing right through them.[25]

When we are judging the degree of relational risk we might be taking, what are the valid concerns that we should weigh? Consider the following marks of "unsafe people," summarized by clinical psychologists Henry Cloud and John Townsend:

> They think they "have it all together" instead of readily admitting their weaknesses.
> They're defensive instead of being open to feedback.
> They apologize without changing their behavior.
> They blame others instead of taking personal responsibility.
> They are more concerned about "I" than about "we."
> They resist freedom instead of encouraging it.
> They flatter us instead of confronting us.
> They condemn us instead of forgiving us.
> They gossip instead of keeping secrets.
> They are a negative influence instead of a positive one.[26]

No one is perfect, and no one is perfectly safe. We all have character flaws. But the Bible encourages us to look deeply at a person's character and to make some assessments about that character before we plunge headlong into a relationship. There are habitually unsafe people in the world, and they must be approached with great caution.

Step 4: Work through the stages of a deepening relationship. Once we are reasonably confident that we've found a safe person, we need to be willing to work through the relational stages. In most relationships, there are five stages, with the first being *attraction.* The beginning of any relationship is an attraction that we intuitively feel toward another person. We share the same sense of humor, we find each other's conversation engaging. There's an immediate chemistry.

But the second stage is *disappointment.* The initial attraction was based on viewing the other person from a relational distance, not up close. When we get to know someone beyond a superficial level, the initial attraction is immediately colored by the person's inevitable weaknesses.

Many relationships are allowed to die when they reach this rude awakening. At times, this is appropriate. We find that lasting chemistry isn't there, certain differences are overwhelming, or the person turns out to be terribly unsafe.

But most of the time the differences that end a relationship are trivial. We don't allow the other person the freedom to be different. We don't grant the grace that allows the other person to make a mistake or two.

Which brings us to the third relational stage, that of *acceptance.* This is when we work through the disappointments and allow ourselves to come to a healthy understanding of someone else's strengths and weaknesses. Then we accept the person on those terms. If we're not able to do this, we'll never have a meaningful relationship. No human is free of things that might disappoint us. If we're unable or unwilling to move into the stage of acceptance, then we'll lead a very lonely and isolated life. The *kairos* nature of knowing and being known will be lost on us. Or as John Powell reflects, "What I am, at any given moment in the process of my becoming a person, will be determined by my relationships with those who love me or refuse to love me, with those whom I love or refuse to love."[27]

But once we've worked through attraction, disappointment, and acceptance, we can move on to the fourth stage, which is *appreciation.* This gets back to what attracted us to the person to begin with. It's the stage at which we appreciate all that is good and wonderful about him. It's from this plateau that we can journey into the most wonderful of worlds, that of *relational intimacy*—the fifth and final stage. This is a land that is wide in its terrain and rich in its bounty. It's also the place where we find life as it's meant to be lived. Intimate friends help each other carve out this deep, rewarding existence.

THE TIME IS NOW

The *kairos* nature of entering into intimacy with others is seldom perceived to be as pressing as the "heavier" issues of facing temptation, finding and granting forgiveness, or many of the other life-defining moments. Only when a relationship is lost, or the fruits of distance and isolation surface, do we come to see the immediate bearing it holds.

In his book *Between Man and Man*, the famous Jewish philosophy professor Martin Buber tells of a student who came to him for counsel. Buber was in his office, extraordinarily busy, in the midst of a writing project. Without really listening, he gave the student a quick dose of professional, competent advice, and dismissed him. Then the student went out and committed suicide.

Buber later reflected on how the incident caused him to search to the core of his being. If he'd been really present, really engaged, really there for that student, would the outcome have been the same? From that day on, he realized the importance of being present where you are.[28]

"To be present is to be vulnerable, to be able to be hurt, to be willing to be spent," writes Douglas Steere, "but it is also to be awake, alive, and engaged actively in the immediate assignment that has been laid upon us."[29]

And that immediate assignment is community with others.

A few years ago a plane went down that carried many of the men and women involved in the band and road crew of country singer Reba McEntire. It was a devastating loss to the recording industry, but even more devastating to those, like Reba, who knew them.

Out of the pain, a song was recorded. It wasn't the typical song of loss and the grief that accompanies it. Instead it dealt with the importance of seizing every chance, no matter how awkward, to reach for intimacy. A chance she and others wished they could have over again with those who had died, offering a gentle reminder to the rest of us to seize the moment we have been given today to connect with those who still are with us. The words speak for themselves.

If I had only known
It was our last walk in the rain
I'd keep you out for hours in the storm
I would hold your hand
Like a life line to my heart
Underneath the thunder we'd be warm
If I had only known
It was our last walk in the rain

If I had only known
I'd never hear your voice again
I'd memorize each thing you ever said
And on those lonely nights
I could think of them once more
Keep your words alive inside my head
If I had only known
I'd never hear your voice again

You were the treasure in my hand
You were the one who always stood beside me

So unaware I foolishly believed
That you would always be there
But then there came a day
And I closed my eyes and you slipped away

If I had only known
It was my last night by your side
I'd pray a miracle would stop the dawn
And when you smiled at me
I would look into your eyes
And make sure you know my love
For you goes on and on
If I had only known
If I had only known
The love I would've shown
If I had only known[30]

3

WHEN FACED WITH FAILURE

Fifteen is, at best, an awkward age. No longer a child, not quite an adult. As a sophomore at Laney High School in Wilmington, North Carolina, a fifteen-year-old was determined to try out for the varsity basketball team.

He didn't have much of a shot. Literally.

Whenever he'd throw the ball toward the hoop, it was as if an invisible hand shoved it aside. No one was surprised when he didn't make the team. What did surprise them was how he reacted to not making the team. Rather than walk away in defeat, he made the decision to practice. A lot. Determined to make his errant shot arc straight to the basket, he spent endless hours in the gym.

Few would deny the life-changing proportions of his decision. The teenager who failed to make the high school team was Michael Jordan.

Failure is a universal experience, transcending time and culture, age and gender, geography and social position. Most defeats in life are far more serious than failing to make a school team. Our lives can become devastated by divorce, bankruptcy, drinking and driving, being fired from a job, flunking out of school, lying, or falling short as a parent.

What is not shared is a common reaction to failure. Yet it is precisely our response to failure, as opposed to the failure itself, that presents a *kairos* moment that holds the potential of shaping our destiny. The widespread awareness of the pivotal nature of this moment was revealed when an article in *Leadership Journal* called for "training in failure."[1] It's not that we need to become more adept in the ways we fail; that seems to happen without our even trying. But we could use training in better ways to respond to the inevitable failures of life.

If failure becomes the final word, all is lost. Emotions become deadened, dreams are allowed to fade, and the will to steadfastly endure and prevail is lost. As the wisdom of Proverbs reminds us, "[A]s he thinks within himself, so he is."[2] Yet when we refuse to allow failure to have the final say, we pull ourselves from the rubble and resolve to change. From this flows the motivation to persevere, giving rise to a flood of new ideas and the assurance of a second chance.

The Bible gives us a practical prescription for just such a course of action. The backdrop is found in Paul's second letter to the Christians in Corinth, where he shares how he dealt with failure in his own life. By his own admission he had experienced:

- prison
- public floggings and lashings
- sickness unto death

- beatings
- a stoning
- shipwrecks
- homelessness and hunger
- intense emotional stress[3]

Yet after each blow, Paul carried on. By the end of his life, he had single-handedly taken the gospel to virtually every corner of the known world while authoring most of the New Testament along the way. His secret? It can be found in two succinct verses, tucked away in his short letter to the church at Philippi: "one thing I do: Forgetting what is behind and straining toward what is ahead, I press on toward the goal to win the prize for which God has called me heavenward in Christ Jesus."[4] These are more than empty words. They represent a life map that enabled Paul to capitalize on the *kairos* nature of his setbacks in such a way that it shaped his very destiny. And the challenge his words bring begins by letting go of the past.

RELEASE THE PAST

Have you ever walked past a circus elephant and wondered how a puny, eighteen-inch stake driven into the ground can secure such a massive beast? Ask an elephant trainer and you'll receive an intriguing answer. All elephants *try* to pull away as babies, but they find they aren't strong enough to dislodge the stake. The elephant then concludes that he can't *ever* pull it out of the ground. Legends of an elephant's long memory aren't exaggerated. Even after the animal is strong enough to pull whole trees out of the ground, it is held captive by a puny, eighteen-inch stake of wood. Or at least the *memory* of it.[5]

Listen to the words of Paul: "I forget all that lies behind me."[6] In reflecting on failure, he chose to let go of the past. Paul doesn't minimize the significance of those failures. And there is nothing within his counsel that would warrant turning our backs on the lessons to be learned from failure or denying the possibility of lingering consequences that may flow from past actions.

Instead, the apostle is speaking to the weight of failure on our souls and the deadly risk of letting our failures have the last word. Just as a lack of forgiveness keeps a perceived offense alive in the present, so focusing on failure keeps us tied down to a negative past. The truth is, what's done is done. We must move on.

But you don't know about my *failure*, you may be thinking. True, and you don't know about mine.

But I do know about God, and He is big enough for all of our failures. If it was a moral failure or failure due to sin or disobedience, we need only remember that the word *forgive* means "to bleach out" or "to forget." That's why the Bible can say, in essence, turn loose of the past; it's forgotten. The heart of God toward our sin and failure is not one of condemnation but reclamation. "For God did not send his Son into the world to condemn the world," Jesus said, "but to save the world."[7] God isn't interested in taking all of our failures and condemning us. He wants to take all of our failures and forgive us—and help us start over.

Whether our failure was simple carelessness, the inability to perform up to standard, or the seemingly random strike of circumstances, we need to refuse to let it define us for the rest of our lives. We can let it become a page in our journal but never a reflection in the mirror.

LAY HOLD OF THE FUTURE

Letting go of the past is only the first part of Paul's life map. The second leg of the journey builds on its foundation, for Paul next commends the practice of "looking forward to what lies ahead."[8] It isn't enough to say, "Well, I blew that one. But I've asked God to forgive me, so that's that." No, the Bible says to now turn your eyes to what lies ahead.

Orienting our lives with an eye to the future doesn't mean that we don't try to learn from our failures and mistakes. We don't merely shove them aside, pretending they never happened. Instead, we consider how we can avoid making the same mistakes in the future. But the key is not to get bogged down in the past. Paul tells us to let go of what's behind us and look forward to all that lies ahead. Yet we are not to simply look to the future but to "press on" toward it. So we are to learn from our past failures, while never allowing them to become a ball and chain that keep us from moving ahead with our lives.

Eddie Robinson, the legendary head football coach at Grambling State University, coached the Tigers through twenty-five consecutive winning seasons. He set a new record as the winningest coach in college football history. When the Tigers suffered a loss to unranked Jackson State, a television sportscaster asked him about the loss, and Robinson simply said that his team hadn't played well.

"But you can't unring the bell," he added. "We've got to begin getting ready for Texas Southern next week." Robinson summarized one of the great insights into seizing the *kairos* opportunity inherent within failure. Let go of the past, for you can never unring the bell, and immediately start getting ready for the next game!

According to the Bible, this can be done with confidence. "I am sure," Paul would write elsewhere, "that God, who began the good work within you, will continue his work until it is finally finished."[9] If you are a Christian, God is working in your life toward a goal. He wants to shape you, mold you, and move you toward His perfect will for your life. Even when you fail, God desires to begin again, right where you are.

Leaders at IBM circulate a story to new employees about the junior executive who was managing an IBM project that had lost ten million dollars before it finally was scrapped. He was called into the office of Tom Watson Sr., the founder and leader of IBM for forty years and one of the great business legends of all time.

When the junior executive was ushered into Watson's office, the younger man said, "I suppose you want my resignation."

"You must be joking!" exclaimed Watson. "I just invested ten million dollars educating you—I can't afford your resignation!"[10]

God doesn't want us to hand in our resignations. He wants to take our failures, have us learn from them, and then move into the future.

But this takes purposeful focus, because not everyone shares God's view of our lives. A schoolteacher told a seven-year-old boy he should drop out of school because he wasn't creative and was virtually unteachable. The boy's name was Thomas Edison, and he went on to create tremendous technologies, inventing such things as the light bulb and the phonograph.[11]

After the first performance of *The Marriage of Figaro,* the Emperor Ferdinand told Mozart that it was "far too noisy" and had "far too many notes."[12]

A Dutchman gave painting a whirl, only to have someone remark that his work would scarcely be remembered. The painter was Rembrandt.[13]

A boy was told he was a poor student, especially in mathematics. Because of his perceived mental slowness and inability to perform, there was an effort to remove him from school. A Munich schoolmaster even went so far as to say the ten-year-old would never amount to much. Albert Einstein's mother was glad they let her little boy stay in school anyway.[14]

In 1962, the Decca recording company told four young lads named John, Paul, George, and Ringo that they didn't like their sound and that groups with guitars were on the way out.

Few will look past our failures and into the future for us. It must be a personal, purposeful choice that we make for ourselves in the confidence of God's dream for our lives. This is not simply walking through life with a positive attitude, but knowing that there is more to be seen than meets the eye.

An economist was asked to talk to a group of business people. She tacked up a big sheet of white paper then drew a black spot on the paper and asked a man in the front row what he saw.

The man replied, "A black spot."

The speaker asked every person in the room the same question, and each one saw only a black spot.

"Yes," the speaker said, "there is a little black spot, but none of you mentioned the big sheet of white paper. And that's my speech."

The past failure in your life is like that little black spot. The future that God not only wants to give to you, but that truly is already here, is the large white sheet of paper.

MOVE AHEAD WITH YOUR LIFE

After forgetting our past failures and looking to what lies ahead, Paul supplies the third dynamic of his life map: "I press on toward the goal to win the prize for which God has called me heavenward in Christ Jesus."[15] While all three course corrections are critical, the difference between failing and being a failure is found right here: Do you press on or not? Lots of people have adjusted to past failures; many have caught a vision of the life that could lie ahead; but not many have truly pressed on.

Consider the life of the most revered U.S. president, Abraham

Lincoln. You may be surprised at the flow of his life. When he was just seven years old, his family was forced out of their home. Young Abraham had to go to work to help provide financial support. When he was nine, his mother died. At twenty-two he lost his job.

He wanted to attend law school but didn't have the necessary education. At twenty-three he borrowed money to become a partner in a small store. Three years later his partner died, leaving him with a huge debt that would take years to repay.

When Lincoln was twenty-eight, he asked the girl he had been dating for four years to marry him. She turned him down. The only other girl he'd ever loved had died several years before.

At thirty-seven, on his third try, he finally was elected to Congress. Two years later he ran again and lost. He then experienced a nervous breakdown.

At age forty-one, in the midst of what already was an unhappy marriage, Lincoln's four-year-old son died. The next year he was rejected again for another public office. At forty-five he ran for the Senate and lost. Two years later he was defeated for the nomination for vice president. At forty-nine, he again ran for the Senate. And once again, he lost.

Only at age fifty-one did Abraham Lincoln finally end his string of failures and become the sixteenth president of the United States, a man of whom it was said at the moment of his dying, "There lies the most perfect ruler of men the world has ever seen."[16]

How did he do it? Like Paul, he pressed on toward the goal. As the defeats fell like rain with every passing year, he deepened his resolve to press on. This same determination is revealed in Paul's letter to the Corinthians:

We are pressed on every side by troubles, but we are not crushed and broken. We are perplexed, but we don't give up and quit. We are hunted down, but God never abandons us. We get knocked down, but we get up again and keep going.[17]

The choice to press on is so critical to the *kairos* moment that we need to get specific about what is needed to enable us to press on. The author of Hebrews elaborates on this theme with great detail and gives us the most compelling blueprint:

[S]ince we are surrounded by such a huge crowd of witnesses to the life of faith, let us strip off every weight that slows us down, especially the sin that so easily hinders our progress. And let us run with endurance the race that God has set before us. We do this by keeping our eyes on Jesus, on whom our faith depends from start to finish. He was willing to die a shameful death on the cross because of the joy he knew would be his afterward. Now he is seated in the place of highest honor beside God's throne in heaven. Think about all he endured when sinful people did such terrible things to him, so that you don't become weary and give up.[18]

The first element of pressing on is to remember others who have set the pace. The Bible says we should take heart by remembering that other people have made it. So can we. Not only are we surrounded by the heroes of the faith, but we have the life of Jesus Himself urging us on.

Calling to mind others who have pressed on is more decisive than you might think. Remember the four-minute mile? People had been trying to achieve this feat of speed since the days of the ancient Greeks. Folklore has it that the Greeks set lions loose to chase the runners, thinking that would make them run faster. They also tried drinking tiger's milk—not the stuff you get at the health food store, but the real thing.

Nothing the Greeks tried worked. They decided it was impossible for a person to run a mile in four minutes or less. For more than a thousand years everyone accepted this assumption as the truth. Our bone structure was all wrong. Wind resistance was too great. We had inadequate lung power.

Then one man, a single human being, proved that the doctors, the trainers, the athletes, and the hundreds of thousands of runners before him who tried and failed were wrong. All it took was for Roger Bannister to press on toward the goal that no one else had been able to achieve.

Incredibly, the year after Bannister did the unthinkable, thirty-seven other milers broke the four-minute mark. The year after that *three hundred* runners broke the barrier. A few years ago, in a single race in New York, thirteen out of thirteen runners ran the race in less than four minutes.[19]

There were no great breakthroughs in training. No one discovered how to control wind resistance. Human bone structure and physiology didn't suddenly mutate. So what changed? People saw that someone else could do it, and they remembered the accomplishments of the others when *they* ran.

The second requirement to pressing on is getting rid of anything that weighs us down or trips us up. Another interesting note about athletic competition in ancient Greece is that they would compete without any clothing to ensure that they were running as fast and unencumbered as possible. It is with this in mind that the Bible tells us, "We should remove from our lives anything that would get in the way and the sin that so easily holds us back."[20]

There are things in our lives that hurt our ability to endure. They slow us down and get in our way. We can be held back by negative people who tell us all the things that we can't possibly do. We can be held back by bad habits or by spreading ourselves so thin that we can't focus on great achievement in a single area. But the biggest hindrance to pressing past our failure is the one mentioned specifically by the biblical writer in Hebrews: our sin.

Sin is a word that means "missing the mark." It is shooting at the target and missing the bull's-eye. It's falling short of God's standard. God designed us to function best when we live in a particular way. It's difficult to be someone who lives life to the fullest, persevering to the end, if destructive activities and less than ideal choices are being made on a regular basis. Habitual patterns of sin, unconfessed and unrepented, bring defeat to our failure. Failures cost us the battle, but ongoing sin will lose the war.

The importance of this was captured by Portia Nelson in *Autobiography in Five Short Chapters.*

Chapter 1. I walk down the street. There is a deep hole in the sidewalk. I fall in. I am lost. I am helpless. It isn't my fault. It takes forever to find a way out.

Chapter 2. I walk down the street. There is a deep hole in the sidewalk. I pretend I don't see it. I fall in again. I can't believe I am in the same place, but it isn't my fault. It still takes a long time to get out.

Chapter 3. I walk down the same street. There is a deep hole in the sidewalk. I see it is there. I still fall in. It's a habit. My eyes are open. I know where I am. It is my fault. I get out immediately.

Chapter 4. I walk down the same street. There is a deep hole in the sidewalk. I walk around it.

Chapter 5. I walk down another street.[21]

It is the fifth chapter that we must finally find. I don't know what's sapping the strength from your ability to endure, but if you are honest with yourself, you probably do, and the Bible says to throw it off, to give it up, to walk away from it. When it comes to ongoing sin, we must walk down another street.

The third and final requirement for successfully pressing on is to run the race with patience. The opening weekend of the church I pastor, Mecklenburg Community Church, was a church planter's nightmare. It was the first Sunday in October 1992. I had all the hopes and dreams of any pioneer. We'd sent out a direct-mail piece to thousands of homes in the surrounding area. The service was planned, the details had been attended to, and now it was time to see hundreds stream in the doors.

Hundreds didn't.

On Sunday, October 4, 1992, the aftermath of Tropical Storm Earl struck the Carolinas. Record-breaking rainfall, thirty-five mph winds, and downed power lines plagued the Charlotte area. Our debut service started at ten, and at five minutes before that hour not a soul had come except for the meager band of volunteers—all on loan from other churches.

I told everyone present that we'd just make it a rehearsal. I even tried to put a good spin on it, telling them that the run-through would make it that much better the following week. Then I went into a small room to pray and broke down. I shook my fist at God and said, "I love You and I trust You, but I don't get it! This was Your idea. You control the weather, and You didn't have to do this!"

After five minutes of exercising incredible maturity in my attitudes, I came out, ready to limp through what I was beginning to feel was a farce. A miraculous group of 112 showed, but I was devastated. Through the strength of my preaching, we were at 56 by the third week. It was apparent that we weren't going to begin the way I had dreamed.

I had to recall the Bible's words: "run with endurance the race that God has set before us."[22] Everything within me wanted to stop, to quit, to give up on the first day, because I had an idea of the race that others had run and wanted that to be my own. But I had to run my own race, the one God had for me. I had to be patient, following His timetable. Today, Mecklenburg Community Church often is cited as one of the fastest-growing new churches in the nation, attracting thousands of attendees every weekend.

And to think that I wanted to quit on the first day.

A runner with even more patience is known simply as Rudy. Those of us who saw the movie that carries his name bonded with a kid who wanted to play football for Notre Dame more than anything in the world. It was based on the story of Daniel "Rudy" Ruettiger, and it turns out his real life was even more exceptional than the film.

He was the first of fourteen children born into a poor, working-class family in Joliet, Illinois. Not a particularly fast athlete, he also was small for the game of football—only five feet six inches tall, weighing in at 190 pounds.

His grades were just as unimpressive. He was a D student and graduated from high school with a 1.77 grade point average. He attended junior college for one semester but flunked every class. He went to work for a couple of years at the local Commonwealth Edison power plant and then did a two-year stint in the U.S. Navy. After his military service, he returned to Joliet to work at the power plant.

Not exactly the route that would land one a roster spot with the Fighting Irish.

But then he quit his job, moved to South Bend, Indiana, and managed to get into Holy Cross College. He attended the college for two years and earned a 4.0 average every semester. He then was accepted to Notre Dame.

The dream that yearned to be fulfilled at eighteen took place at twenty-six. But the dream came true.

With two years of sports eligibility remaining, he tried out for the football team, which he made as a "scrub," one of the warm bodies put into practice to keep the "real" players sharp. But Rudy worked hard, kept at it, and slowly rose from the bottom of the scrubs up to the sixth string—the top of the scrubs.

In the final game of his final season, Rudy achieved his lifelong dream by getting to play. In the movie, he got in for only one play and sacked the quarterback. In truth, he was in for two plays, and on the first he failed miserably. But Rudy didn't let his failure make *him* a failure. On the next play, he got to the quarterback. For the first time in the history of Notre Dame football, a player was carried off of the field on the shoulders of his teammates.[23]

RUNNING TO THE END

Almost twenty thousand runners competed in the 1986 New York City Marathon. The person who finished last was a man named Bob Wieland. It took him four days, two hours, forty-eight minutes, and seventeen seconds. It was the slowest recorded marathon time in history.

But Bob finished it, which is what mattered. Even though it meant running with his arms.

Seventeen years earlier, in Vietnam, Bob's legs were blown off in battle. To run, Bob had to cover his fists with pads and run with his arms. He averaged about one mile an hour. Why'd he do it? Because Bob knew that the real issue wasn't how fast you can run or the setbacks along the way. It's whether you have what it takes to finish the race.[24]

We can succeed in pressing on if we lay hold of the three essentials. First, remember others who have set the pace. Second, get rid of anything that weighs us down or trips us up. Third, run the race with endurance. When these three work together in our lives, failures can't defeat us. When these three work together, we receive the full benefit of this *kairos* moment.

4

WHEN PURSUING YOUR PURPOSE

He was on *The Mike Douglas Show* at age three, demonstrating his uncanny ability to hit a golf ball off the tee and to putt from a distance. As he grew, he put pictures of golf legend Jack Nicklaus on his wall, memorizing every major record the greatest golfer up to that time had ever held. After winning a tournament, he'd retire to a driving range to improve on whatever element of his game had been lacking. It's difficult to imagine someone living with more single-minded purpose than Tiger Woods. At the time of this writing, he has won all four majors and has broken virtually every record in the annals of golf.

But it's one thing to *set* a course and follow it. It's quite another to *find* your course and follow it. The essence of a life truly lived is summed up in the Bible's epitaph for one of the greatest human lives ever lived, that of King David. The Scriptures simply but profoundly say, "David...served God's purpose in his own generation."[1] Whenever we serve God's purpose, we enter into a *kairos* moment that is seized by God in a way that does nothing less than change the world.

William Wilberforce was a member of the English Parliament in the late eighteenth century. He'd become a Christian through some of John Wesley's early disciples. His Christian life infused him with a sense of personal purpose, and he seized it.

Wilberforce found his purpose in life sparked by his outrage over the slave trade. Among the most barbaric of practices, Africans were packed in slave ships like cargo and carried off to the Western Hemisphere, many dying en route. Sacrificing an opportunity to become Britain's prime minister, Wilberforce challenged the political leadership of his day to end the slave trade. He began his great campaign in 1787. Year after year his efforts were defeated in Parliament, but he pressed on. He never despaired and never counted the odds against him, because he knew what his life was about.

Finally, after a twenty-year struggle, a majority voted in the House of Commons to end the unconscionable practices of the slave trade. Twenty-five years later, when Wilberforce was on his deathbed, slavery itself was abolished throughout the British Empire.[2]

Few would deny the *kairos* nature of finding and then following a life purpose. Doing so would be the fulfillment of one's highest destiny. What hinders us is our difficulty in believing that we have a destiny to fulfill. Responsibilities? Yes. A great purpose bequeathed to us, founded in the very creation of our being? Well, we just can't see it. We can't help but believe that such things are left to an elite group—the most select lives that God picks out of the masses to have a special role in unique times and events.

But this says more about the way we see things than it does about what is truly there to be seen.

Helen Keller, a woman born deaf and blind and whose story was told through the stage and film presentation of *The Miracle Worker*, was asked what would be worse than being born blind. She answered, "To have sight without vision." Jesus went out of His way to expand people's perspective—not only about the kingdom of God but also about what God wanted to do with their lives. "You're tied down to the mundane," Jesus once said. "I'm in touch with what is beyond your horizons. You live in terms of what you see and touch. I'm living on other terms. I told you that you were missing God in all this. You're at a dead end.... You're missing God in your lives."[3]

You were given life because God had a dream for you. Individually, specifically, by name. You were no accident. God willed you into existence, and He not only gave you life, but He also invested you with promise and potential. Within you is the opportunity to join with God in fulfilling the great adventure birthed in His mind for you from eternity.

But just because you were created in the context of this divine plan, is it a requirement that you fulfill your purpose? Certainly not.

During that pivotal moment of Jewish history when the evil Haman of Persia plotted to kill the Jews in a holocaust-style extermination, Mordecai went to the Queen of Persia—Esther, herself a Jew—to intervene. She understandably balked at this high-risk proposal. Mordecai's reply is captivating: "If you remain silent at this time, relief and deliverance for the Jews will arise from another place…[yet] who knows but that you have come to royal position for such a time as this?"[4] God's great purposes *will* be fulfilled, with or without our involvement.

In one of the best-known verses in the Bible, we read, "Where there is no vision, the people perish."[5] The Hebrew word for "perish" doesn't mean death in the physical sense but to become purposeless, to run wild, to lose focus. It speaks of a life without goals, without conviction, without priorities, without direction. Failing to find and follow our life purpose not only removes us from the playing field of God's great contest, but it leaves us with a life empty of true meaning.

There are people who get up in the morning, go to work, come home, spend time with their family, go to bed—and don't know why. Maybe you're one of them. You don't know why you're working so hard, why you're married and trying to be committed to that marriage, or why you're investing yourself as a parent. You know the answer on a superficial level. You're working to make money. You stay married because you value commitment and it often is more practical and best for the kids to stay together. But you don't know why you're living your life in an *ultimate* sense.

It's tough to keep working, giving, pushing, and sacrificing without knowing what it's all for in the end. So how can we seize this moment that defines all of life, ensuring that we indeed will find and follow God's purpose for our days? I could easily fill an entire book with the answer to that question—and have—but for now let's consider the following three journeys to self-discovery.[6]

UNDERSTAND WHO YOU ARE FOUNDATIONALLY

Few would argue that the most cherished children's story throughout the world is, in one version or another, "Cinderella." We love to read about someone who's had a difficult life and then becomes highly valued in spite of her background and her poverty. And not only is she valued, but she is brought to the ball, making such an impression that she is sought out by the prince and, in the end, made a princess.

I had a friend who used to tell that story, only he did it in a unique way. He'd tell it with the letters rearranged.

Once upon a time, there lived a girl named Rindercella. She lived with her three sigly usters and her sean mepstother.

One day, they received an invitation from the pransome hince to go to a bancy fall. She went to the bancy fall and danced with the pransome hince. But then the clock muck stridnight, and she had to leave. But as she left, she slopped her dripper. The pransome hince was sery vad. But then he found the slopped dripper and sent his men throughout the kingdom to find her.

A man came to Rindercella's house with the slopped dripper and tried it on her first sigly uster. Find't dit.

Then he tried it on her second sigly uster. Find't dit her, either.

Then he tried it on Rindersella, and it fid dit. She married the pransome hince, and they lived happily ever after.

E thend.

While we love that story, in *almost* any version, we don't think it ever could happen—at least not to us.

Larry Crabb writes about a therapist who used to assemble a group and play a game he called Top Secret. He'd ask the people to write out the one thing about themselves that they were the least inclined to share, the one thing nobody knew about them, and then to return the paper unsigned. Over the years, one answer consistently emerged as the most frequently admitted top secret: "I feel utterly worthless. No one would want me if they knew me."[7]

There can be little sense of ultimate purpose apart from a foundational identity and a clear sense of self-worth. Who *are* you? The Bible says you are a precious child of God. "Consider the incredible love that the Father has shown us in allowing us to be called 'children of God,'" wrote the apostle John. "[A]nd that is not just what we are called, but what we *are*."[8]

There's something special about the relationship between a loving father and his child. It's overpowering. It's irrational. I'll never forget when I first felt that love for my older son, Jonathan. My wife, Susan, needed to get a sonogram relatively late in her pregnancy, and up until then we had no idea whether we were going to have our first boy or a third girl. I was kind of pulling for a girl. I knew girls and understood girls. My wife and daughters had trained me well.

I knew that if we had a son, it would be a journey into the unknown. I didn't know if I'd feel for him the same tender way I felt toward my daughters. And would he feel for me the same way my girls did? When the images first came on the screen, we saw the head, the little feet and hands, and then the nurse said, "Do you want to know whether your baby is a boy or a girl?" We already had talked about it and said, "Yeah, we do."

"Well, it looks like it's a boy!" she said. Then turning to me, she added, "You're going to have a son."

I'll never forget the wave of emotion that swept over me. I instantly had a love for that little guy that was almost overwhelming. My fears and anxieties vanished. All I had was a staggering amount of love for my son. I'd never held him, heard his voice, or called him by name. I didn't even know what his name was going to be. It didn't matter whether he was male or female, white or black, healthy or sick. He was my child, and that was all that mattered. I *loved* him.

That's the way God feels toward you and me. We are His children, and He wants us to live that way! As a son or daughter of God, we are unique, special, and filled with purpose. Our self-image and sense of worth are rooted in our parentage. You are a child of the King, and His fatherly love for you is irrational. It knows no bounds. And it is yours simply because you are His child.

UNDERSTAND WHO YOU
ARE POSITIONALLY

At the foundational level, you are a child of God, and your identity is based on that fact. But *positionally* where are you with that relationship? According to the Bible, we can be intimately related to God the Father, or we can be totally estranged from Him. The reason for that is that our sin has made us runaways.

Author Philip Yancey helps us imagine the feelings that God has in response to our rebellion, as revealed by the great Old Testament prophets. If we were to place God in a counselor's office as a client, the counselor might say, "Tell me how you really feel."

God might answer: "I'll tell you how I feel! I feel like a parent who finds a baby girl lying in a ditch, near death. I take the girl home and make her my daughter. I clean her, pay for her schooling, feed her. I dote on her, clothe her, hang jewelry on her. Then one day she runs away.

"I hear reports of her life of debauchery. She's a drug addict somewhere, covered with tattoos, her body pierced with jewelry. When my name comes up, she curses me. I feel like she's twisting a knife in my stomach…

"I feel betrayed, abandoned…"[9]

That observation is true: We are in fact rebellious children. And yet what is God's response? He continues to love us. He will do anything to restore the broken relationship and have us come home. He even went as far as dying on a cross for us. Through Christ we not only can receive forgiveness, but we once again can enter into the intimacy of God's fatherly love for us. We can be received back into the family. We can come home and be who we are meant to be—sons and daughters. We can come home and allow Him to be who He yearns to be—our Father. As God Himself declared, "I will be a Father to you, and you will be my sons and daughters."[10]

Seizing the *kairos* nature of this moment involves finding and following your purpose. And following that purpose hinges on being actively fathered by God as a son or daughter.

Many people have never been fathered. Biologically, yes, but relationally, no. Many have never received a father's love, care, or support. I don't think there is any pain greater, any emptiness bigger, than that which comes when a child feels emotionally fatherless. Rather than finding and following our purpose, we invest our lives in a vain search for that which will bring about the love, acceptance, and achievement that should have flowed from our earthly father's heart. Our purpose becomes finding those things that a father should have given us rather than taking what a father gave and using it to follow our God-given purpose.

An earthly father is the one person we really need to give us a solid foundation, to put his arms around us, to tell us there's nothing we can't do, and to pick us up when we stumble. We need him sitting on the sidelines, cheering from the grandstands, encouraging us and watching out for our well-being. We yearn for his counsel, his direction, even his boundaries and rebukes. We depend on his provision, the secure foundation he provides to enable us to reach for the stars.

We do, in fact, have that kind of Father, One who loves us with all His heart. He gives us all good things because we are His precious sons and daughters. God wants to care for us, to provide for us, to lead and guide us, to cheer us on and to mentor us, to teach us. "God is educating you.... He's treating you as dear children," writes the author of Hebrews. "Only irresponsible parents leave children to fend for themselves...so why not embrace God's training so we can truly *live?*... God is doing what *is* best for us, training us to live God's holy best."[11]

Yet our willful spirits often lead us into rebellion. Instead of welcoming the fathering activity of God, we orphan ourselves. The only way to have God as Father is to submit ourselves to Him as child. And as Frederick Buechner reminds us, children "live with their hands open more than with their fists clenched."[12]

UNDERSTAND WHO YOU ARE INDIVIDUALLY

The close of the twentieth century was marked by the race to decode the human genetic code. The Human Genome Project was the most expensive, most ambitious biology mission in history. It's been called biology's equivalent to NASA's moonshot. It's goal? Nothing less than creating an operating manual with comprehensive instructions for the human body. With that knowledge, we're now able to revolutionize the detection, prevention, and treatment of conditions from cancer to depression to old age itself.[13]

But what if there were a deeper "spiritual DNA," one that allowed us to peer even further inside who we really are? There is. You inherited your genetic makeup from your biological parents, but you also inherited unique characteristics as a result of being a child of God.

Because you are intimately related to your heavenly Father, you've been given a unique identity that is shared with no one else. Within the context of your relationship with God as Father, you are to pursue the life He has given you in light of the person He created you to be. That spiritual identity is found deeply within, far deeper than anything the Human Genome Project will ever unravel. The quest to find your spiritual genetic code involves three questions:

- What are your gifts and abilities?
- What is your personality type?
- What are your passions?

All three must be considered, beginning with the one the apostle Paul was most adamant about—identifying and using our unique spiritual gifts. He wrote: "Christ has given each of us special abilities—whatever he wants us to have out of his rich storehouse of gifts."[14] In another place, he asserted: "God has given each of us the ability to do certain things well."[15]

So ask yourself these questions: What are my gifts and abilities? What do I do well? What comes easily to me? What do I really enjoy?

The second question is often more complex but equally critical: "What is your personality type?" There can be little doubt that each of us has a specific and unique personality. It's how God intended it to be. This is one of the meanings within the great tribute to the precious sanctity of life in Psalm 139: "For you [God] created my inmost being."[16]

Some of us are introverts by nature; others are wildly extroverted. Regardless, determining your purpose in life will involve understanding how God wired you.

The final question you need to consider is "What do you *feel* strongly about?"

When my younger son was two years old, he felt *very* strongly about a certain purple dinosaur named Barney. We had Barney toys, Barney videos, and Barney underwear.

I developed a passion about Barney, too, but it wasn't along the same emotional currents of my son. I came very close to joining the secret I Hate Barney Society (yes, it's real). The club's motto is You Don't Have to Tell Your Kids You Belong. The theme song: "I hate you, you hate me. Let's hang Barney from a tree." Okay, I know I'm terrible. But you have to at least agree that Baby Bop has got to go.[17]

In truth, the issue is not simply strong feelings, but strong *passions.* Consider the question from this angle: "If you could do something that would make every day feel like Christmas, what would it be?" God is more interested in that answer than we often imagine. As the psalmist reminds us, "Delight yourself in the LORD and he will give you the desires of your heart. Commit your way to the LORD; trust in him and he will do this."[18]

My friend Rick Warren, who pastors Saddleback Valley Community Church in California, uses an acrostic built on the word *shape* that offers a good summary of all three questions.

S stands for our spiritual gifts, those special capabilities to be used for God's kingdom that He gives us when we enter into a relationship with Him.

H stands for our heart or our passions, those things that bring about burning intensity and enthusiasm. These are the things that interest us, that we care about, that draw us.

A stands for our abilities, those natural talents and skills that we were born with.

P stands for our personality, whether we are an extrovert or an introvert, a thinker or a feeler.

E stands for our experiences. This includes our educational and vocational background, as well as the unique experiences we've had that have molded our lives.[19]

God has given you your shape, and He wants to use you *according* to your shape. Much of your purpose will involve simply doing what you are. Some of you have the shape of a leader, others have the shape of a teacher, a counselor, an artist, a musician, an administrator, or a caregiver. There is no end to the number of shapes, for God is the God of limitless individuality.

DON'T HOLD BACK

Journeys that lead to self-discovery won't take us very far if they are divorced from the ultimate journey—that of choosing to *follow* our life purpose with abandon. As Paul reminds us, the goal is to put ourselves into play according to our God-given purpose.[20]

I watched a film called *Gattaca* during a long commercial flight. It was a futuristic thriller about what life might be like when genetic engineering becomes commonplace. While it presented a fascinating look at where genetic research might take us, I was much more taken by the spirit of the main character.

In the genetically enhanced world, he was an outcast. Born with normal defects and weaknesses, he hadn't benefited from the advances afforded other children. In that futuristic world, his imperfections forced him to the lowest levels of education, employment, and opportunity. But he knew his life was meant for more.

By submitting black market urine and blood samples, he entered the genetically ordered system with a disguised identity, pursuing his dream of leaving earth in the pursuit of astro-science, an opportunity only given to the best and the brightest humans that genetic engineering could produce. And despite his deficiencies, he rose to the top.

There was a reason.

Although his brother had benefited from genetic enhancement, the kind that would open doors and allow him unlimited advancement, he had achieved very little. Throughout their time together as children, the genetically engineered brother continually lost out to his "deficient" brother, illustrated in a contest they pursued time and again. They'd stand on the edge of the ocean, look each other in the eye, and then begin to swim. The challenge was to see who'd be the first to turn around and swim back. They both knew if they went too far and didn't have the strength to return, they'd drown. It was a test of courage, physical strength, and stamina. The brother who'd been genetically graced always turned back first.

Toward the end of the movie, as adults, they engaged in this contest one last time. The younger, supposedly weaker, brother prevailed once again. In the middle of the ocean, as he was forced to return, the bested brother said, "How do you swim so far? How do you do it? How have you always done it?"

With shocking intensity, the younger brother answered, "I never leave anything for the swim back. I never have."

Finding your life purpose is a *kairos* moment, but it's squandered if you don't pursue your purpose with passion. Following your life purpose demands wholesale abandon, risk, sacrifice, and radical trust in the loving heart of the living God. It calls us to swim out from shore without leaving anything for the swim back.

But it's the swim to greatness.

5

WHEN TAKING A STAND

It was a simple cross marked out in rough stones and set in the middle of Broad Street opposite Balliol College. It was my first visit to the "city of dreaming spires," otherwise known as Oxford, England. It seemed an odd sort of marking in the middle of the road. I would soon discover that it was as close to a holy place as I would find in the entire city.

Thomas Cranmer was born the son of a village squire in Nottinghamshire on July 2, 1489. Little did his parents guess that by 1533 he would be appointed archbishop of Canterbury by Henry VIII and become the unchallenged leader of the English Reformation. His *Book of Common Prayer,* published during the reign of Henry's son, Edward VI, together with the King James Authorized Version of the Bible, were the twin texts upon which three hundred years of the British Empire were built.

Cranmer was not alone in his efforts. Two men—Nicholas Ridley, the bishop of London, and Hugh Latimer, the bishop of Worcester—stood by his side. Together they swept away questionable practices and unfounded doctrines to try to unearth the pillars of Reformation thought: *sola scriptura, sola gratia, sola fidei.* Scripture alone, grace alone, faith alone. Then another revolution took place. Edward VI died, and the will of Henry VIII made the very *non*-Reformation-minded Mary next in line for the throne, a woman known throughout history as Bloody Mary.

She came by her nickname the old-fashioned way: She earned it.

Upon Edward's death Mary claimed the crown. Lady Jane Grey, queen for a paltry nine days in a futile attempt to thwart Mary's reign, was beheaded at the Tower of London. In March 1554, Mary rounded up the leaders of the English Reformation, including Cranmer, Ridley, and Latimer, and packed them off to Oxford. There, she plotted, they would be exposed as heretics.

One by one, the bishops argued their beliefs in the divinity school. All three later were told in Saint Mary Magadalen Church that it had been determined they were in error. Each was given the chance to recant, and each refused. Under Bloody Mary's leadership, Parliament quickly passed an act reviving the traditional punishment for heretics: burning at the stake.

As an archbishop, Cranmer had an additional trial to endure. He was locked in the Bocardo prison from which he was forced to watch as Latimer and Ridley, after a much swifter trial, were taken to the stake outside the city wall. Just before his death, Latimer uttered a cry that has echoed across the centuries: "Be of good comfort, Master Ridley, and play the man! We shall this day light such a candle, by God's grace, in England, as I trust never shall be put out."

And it wasn't.

The simple cross set in the middle of Broad Street marks the spot where these men were burned. To this day, when repairs are made to the thoroughfare, the spot is left untouched and unpaved. It's a sacred place that marks a sacred moment.[1]

Taking a stand for what is right is one of the most *kairos*-filled points of time in any person's life. Choosing to do so can, as we've seen, hasten your death. Yet failing to do so can keep you from the essence of life. All *kairos* moments afford a gateway to lasting consequence, but taking a stand sweeps you into the great drama of living.

In J. R. R. Tolkien's epic *The Lord of the Rings,* the elderly hero of an earlier adventure, Bilbo Baggins, offers to carry the Ring of Power into the Dark Lord's domain. Once there, he intends to cast it into the fire in which it was made. Musing to himself, the hero was heard to say, "Bilbo the silly hobbit started this affair, and Bilbo had better finish it, or himself."

The hobbit is gently released from the task by his old friend, Gandalf the wizard. "If you had really started this affair," Gandalf told him, "you might be expected to finish it. But you know well enough now that *starting* is too great a claim for any, and that only a small part is played in great deeds by any hero."[2]

The great starter of events, of course, is God Himself. And while the great deeds are not done by a few, but by many, the heroes are bound by their choice to take a stand. Through this decision, they assume a role in the great contest between good and evil; between the movement of God and the rebellion of the Evil

One. Each succeeding generation carries on, playing its part in the great cosmic battle that eventually will be brought to a finish at the end of history. The question is whether we will choose to walk in the footsteps of the heroes who went before us. It's a daunting choice indeed.

In *The Lord of the Rings,* Bilbo's young cousin Frodo had to decide whether to carry on the adventure his older relative had so faithfully pursued throughout his life. And choose he did.

> "I will take the Ring," he said, "though I do not know the way."
>
> Elrond raised his eyes and looked at him, and Frodo felt his heart pierced by the sudden keenness of the glance. "If I understand aright all that I have heard," he said, "I think that this task is appointed for you, Frodo; and that if you do not find a way, no one will. This is the hour of the Shire-folk, when they arise from their quiet fields to shake the towers and counsels of the great. Who of all the Wise could have foreseen it? Or, if they are wise, why should they expect to know it, until the hour has struck?"[3]

The reality and import of such a moment is not simply revealed through fantasy or myth. We all have our defining moments when we are given the opportunity to take a stand that will catapult us onto a brightly lit stage that is much larger than the one constructed for the playing out of our lives. But it can't simply be a moment that is discerned; it must be seized.

Sitting in my study is a small brass bust of Winston Churchill. I purchased the sculpture at Churchill's birthplace, Blenheim Palace, in England. It reminds me of a life that reflected passion, resolve, and deep, deep conviction. Almost single-handedly, Churchill resisted one of the greatest onslaughts of evil the world ever has known, willing the world to victory.

His words to the English people, particularly during that dark summer of 1940, still stir the human heart:

> Hitler knows that he will have to break us in this Island or lose the war. If we can stand up to him, all Europe may be free and the life of the world may move forward into broad, sunlit uplands. But if we fail, then the whole world, including the United States, including all that we have known or cared for, will sink in to the abyss of a new Dark Age made more sinister, and perhaps more protracted, by the lights of perverted science. Let us therefore brace ourselves to our duties and so bear ourselves that if the British Empire and its Commonwealth last for a thousand years men will still say, "This was their finest hour."[4]

Later, biographers would call it *his* finest hour. "In the whole of recorded history this was, I believe, the one occasion when one man, with one soaring imagination, with one fire burning in him, and with one unrivalled capacity for conveying it to others, won a crucial victory...for the very spirit of human freedom," voiced Sir Robert Menzies at Churchill's funeral at Saint Paul's Cathedral in

London. "And so, on this day, we thank him, and we thank God for him."[5]

Compare this to the confession of Martin Niemoller, the German pastor who initially sent a telegram congratulating Hitler on his rise to power:

> In Germany they came first for the communists, and I didn't speak up because I wasn't a communist. Then they came for the Jews, and I didn't speak up because I wasn't a Jew. Then they came for the trade unionists, and I didn't speak up because I wasn't a trade unionist. Then they came for the Catholics, and I didn't speak up because I was a Protestant. Then they came for me, and by that time no one was left to speak up.[6]

Who will speak up today? It's a more pressing question than we might realize. Kay Haugaard, a college professor in southern California, reported an experience in *The Chronicle of Higher Education* that she could only describe as chilling. Her twenty students were discussing Shirley Jackson's short story "The Lottery." Set in a small town in rural America, the townsfolk gather for a ritual deemed critical for the well-being of the crops and the community. At the center of attention is the lottery. Suddenly the story reveals the frightening reality that the people are holding a drawing in preparation for a human sacrifice. In the end, a woman draws the slip of paper marked by a black spot. Stones are gathered, she is encircled, and soon she is dead. Even her small son had pebbles in his hand.

When the *New Yorker* first published this essay in 1948, it was met by a storm of outrage. The story's moral—the danger of blindly "going along" in social conformity—was repugnant to the generation that had stood up to Hitler. But times change. On the warm California night when Haugaard presented the story for discussion, her students registered no moral outrage whatsoever. "The end was neat!" one woman offered. "If it's a part of a person's culture...and if it has worked for them," another suggested.

"At this point I gave up," wrote the professor. "No one in the whole class of twenty ostensibly intelligent individuals would go out on a limb and take a stand against human sacrifice."[7]

Jesus wanted His followers to seize every opportunity to take a stand that would influence the world, and in so doing, mark their own lives as well. Nowhere did this come out more clearly than in His famed Sermon on the Mount, recorded by Matthew. Within the immortal words of this discourse, the Son of God talked of lives that would be composed of two critical elements, both convictional in nature and vigorous in practice.

> You are the salt of the earth. But if the salt loses its saltiness, how can it be made salty again? It is no longer good for anything, except to be thrown out and trampled by men.
>
> You are the light of the world. A city on a hill cannot be

hidden. Neither do people light a lamp and put it under a bowl. Instead they put it on its stand, and it gives light to everyone in the house. In the same way, let your light shine before men, that they may see your good deeds and praise your Father in heaven.[8]

How do you take a stand? Jesus said, "You become the salt of the earth and the light of the world."

THE SALT OF THE EARTH

In Jesus' day salt was one of the most useful and important elements you could possess, but it wasn't because of what it did for the taste of food. The main use for salt was as a preservative. There were no refrigerators or freezers. You couldn't buy things in cans. So salt was used to keep food from spoiling. If you had a piece of meat that you couldn't eat right away, you'd get some salt and rub it in. And that salt, if properly applied, would keep the meat from decaying.[9]

When Jesus said we should live a life that was like salt to the earth, He meant that we should live life in such a way that our very presence in the world *acted* like salt. Though seemingly small, collectively, it would keep the culture from decaying.

In the 1980s New York City was in the grip of one of the worst crime epidemics in its history. But then, from a high in 1990, the crime rate went into a dramatic decline. The murder rate dropped by two-thirds. Felonies were cut in half. Why? The most intriguing explanation is the Broken Windows theory, the brainchild of criminologists James Q. Wilson and George Kelling. They argue that crime is the inevitable result of disorder. If a window is broken and left unrepaired, people walking by will conclude that no one cares and no one's in charge. Soon more windows will be broken, and the sense of anarchy will spread from the building to the street it faces, sending a signal that anything goes. The idea is that crime is contagious. It can start with a broken window and quickly spread to an entire community. When it comes to curtailing crime, what matters is little things, little stands that send a message and chip away at the spread of lawlessness.

That's exactly how New York City addressed the problem. A war was waged on broken windows and graffiti. The cleanup took from 1984 to 1990. It began in the subways and soon spread to the entire city. Law enforcement authorities addressed the seemingly little things, such as turnstile-jumping on the subways, the "squeegee men" who approached drivers at intersections, public drunkenness, and littering. And crime began to fall in the city.[10]

When we live like salt, with lives infused by Christ, it impacts the world around us in disproportionate measure. We are the mended windows and the scrubbed-off graffiti. John Stott rightly notes, "One can hardly blame unsalted meat for going bad. It cannot do anything else. The real question to ask is: where is the salt?"[11]

THE LIGHT OF THE WORLD

Salt is essential in protecting a society against decay, but it's not the only preservative. Jesus also called people to be the light of the world.

The Greek philosopher Plato once told a story about a cave. Imagine, he suggested, that there were men who had lived in a cave from childhood. Their legs and necks have been in chains, preventing them from moving around and seeing what is behind them. As a result, they have spent their entire lives looking at the back of the cave.

Then, Plato continued, imagine that behind them near the mouth of the cave is a fire, throwing shadows on the back wall of the cave. They can't see the fire, for they are chained. All they see, and all that they know, are the shadows dancing in the darkness. The only way for them to see beyond the darkness, to learn the truth about their shadow world, would be to see the light.[12]

Whereas salt is about taking a stand, light is about disclosing what is real. It penetrates the darkness and shows the way. It helps people see beyond the shadows. It can't help but speak.

In the autumn of 1955, five young men dared to make contact with a Stone Age tribe deep in the jungles of Ecuador. Their goal was to establish communication, and through that communication share Christ. These five men were missionaries.

After several preliminary overtures of friendship, they set out in January 1956 for a meeting with the Waorani tribesmen, more popularly known as the Aucas. With their young wives sitting by a two-way radio, Nate Saint, Roger Youderian, Ed McCully, Pete

Fleming, and Jim Elliot made contact with some tribesmen. Soon after that they were slaughtered.

The world was in shock. Images of the bodies of five young men, lying in pools of blood, having been ambushed and cut down with spears, left no one unmoved. But instead of bitterness or revenge, their deaths sparked a missionary movement unlike few others. Stirred by the story of the martyrdom in Ecuador, thousands poured into the mission field, and countless more felt their lives challenged by the commitment of those men to be the light of the world. As one of the men, Jim Elliot, wrote before his death, "He is no fool who gives what he cannot keep to gain what he cannot lose."

Billy Graham convened an international gathering of evangelists in Amsterdam during the summer of 2000, which I had the good fortune of attending. The story of the five missionaries was retold, and then something happened that no one expected. We met their killer.

His name is Minkayi. He led the band of tribesmen that day in January 1956. He was very frank, as he spoke through a translator, about "spearing" the five men. He talked of the blackness in his heart, the hatred he felt toward others, and the lack of feeling he had regarding the death of the men. He also spoke of his life today.

After the five young missionaries were martyred, the effort to reach the Aucas continued. The New Testament was translated in their language. Other missionaries took their lives into their hands and attempted to make contact. Eventually, the blood of those martyrs became the seed of faith. The tribe that once stabbed into the hearts of God's messengers found God's message piercing the depth of their own hearts. Minkayi, the man who killed the five missionaries, shared how he had become a Christian and how Christ had changed his life.

But there is more to the story. The man who was serving as Minkayi's translator in Amsterdam was none other than Steve Saint, the son of slain missionary Nate Saint. In a quiet voice, Steve simply added that this man who killed his father and took away his children's grandfather was now the adopted grandfather to his children and his closest and dearest friend.

At the end Steve wanted to show Minkayi what the bearers of light to his tribe had accomplished—not only in their lives, but around the world. Asking those to stand whose lives were impacted by the five young missionaries, thousands of evangelists from more than two hundred countries rose to their feet.

Think about the effect of light when it is shone into strongholds of spiritual darkness. Five men took it upon themselves to be the light of the world in the darkest corner of Ecuador. A tribe of people came to Christ. And a world was changed.[13]

THE COLUMBINE STORY

When taking a stand, the *kairos* moment is singular in its repercussions. If we refuse to seize this moment, Christ says we are relegating our life to the margins of meaninglessness. The salt must be salty, the light must continue to shine.

"[I]f the salt loses its saltiness," warned Jesus, "how can it be made salty again? It is no longer good for anything, except to be thrown out and trampled by men."[14] Like all *kairos* moments, taking a stand is something that must be done, not just considered. Jesus' challenge on this issue is clear. Each affirmation in the original Greek sentence begins with the emphatic pronoun *you,* as if to say, "You and only you" are the earth's salt; "you and only you" are the world's light. And therefore you simply must not fail the world you are called to serve or the moment you have been given to seize.[15]

On March 8, 1997, a young girl named Cassie became a Christian. At the end of that summer, growing daily in her new-found faith, Cassie went to her parents with a strange request. "Mom, I can't witness to the kids at Christian school. I could reach out to many more people if I were in a public one."

So between her freshman and sophomore years, Cassie's parents let her transfer from her Christian school to one where she might witness to others. She enrolled at Columbine High School in Littleton, Colorado.

Cassie's faith continued to grow. On June 28, 1998, she mused to a friend, "I wonder what God is going to do with my life. Like my purpose. Some people become missionaries and things, but what about me?... For now, I'll just take it day by day.... Maybe I'll look back on my life and think, 'Oh, so that was it!' Isn't it amazing, this plan we're a part of?"

In another letter, dated fall 1998, Cassie reflected, "I know I need to give it all to Christ.... I can't make compromises. It's like being luke-warm." So strong did her faith become that she wrote,

"I will die for my God. I will die for my faith. It's the least I can do for Christ dying for me."

In the spring of her junior year, on the morning of April 20, 1999, Cassie went to school. She handed her friend Amanda a note that ended with "P.S. Honestly, I want to live completely for God. It's hard and scary, but totally worth it." About 11:15 A.M., she walked into the library, backpack on her shoulder, to work on a homework assignment. She was soon followed by two other students—Eric Harris and Dylan Klebold. But instead of backpacks, they carried guns. When the shooters entered the room, students scattered under desks and behind bookcases. Cassie dived under a table and began to pray.

The boys walked up to Cassie, and apparently as a result of seeing her praying, asked, "Do you believe in God?" In the aftermath of this horrific incident, there has been some debate about exactly what happened next. But witnesses have said that in a voice that was not shaky, but strong, Cassie told her self-appointed executioners "Yes." Without a word, they shot her at point-blank range. Before the rampage ended, the two boys turned the guns on themselves. But not before killing thirteen others, including Cassie.

Why, when guns were blazing and fellow students were falling, did Cassie answer in a way that would merit certain death?

Author Madeleine L'Engle has an answer. "Cassie could not have answered that question if she had not already asked it of herself many times and answered Yes many times, and each time answered it affirmatively. The Yes came deeper and deeper from her heart and mind and soul, so deep that she could say Yes even though it endangered her life. And, in the end, cost her her life."[16]

Or did it?

Kairos moments are never pragmatic moves to ensure a blessed life during our short tenure on earth. They are moments to be seized for the sake of eternity and for the Lord of eternity. The call on *every* life is to say Yes. No matter what the cost, it's a small price to pay for what we gain, which is eternal life itself, regardless of when its earthly season ends.

6

WHEN ENGAGED IN SUFFERING

Holocaust survivor Elie Wiesel put the horrors of his experience into words in a recollection aptly titled *Night*. One nightmare evoked from the past describes the hanging of a young boy suspected of sabotage in a Nazi death camp. First, the German Gestapo tortured the boy. When he would not confess, they sentenced him to death with two other prisoners, soon leading all three in chains to the gallows.

It was to be a public execution, with thousands of prisoners watching. The head of the camp read the verdict. All eyes, however, were on the child. He was pale, biting his lips. No more than twelve years old, the boy had the face of a sad angel. The three victims stood on chairs so their necks could be placed within the nooses. The child was silent.

Suddenly someone behind Wiesel cried out, "Where is God? Where is He?"

The executioner tipped the three chairs over, the bodies dropped and then jerked at the end of the ropes. On the horizon, the sun set. Only one noise dared break the silence. It was the sound of men weeping.

The two adults died instantly. Their tongues hung swollen, tinged with blue. But the third rope, the one holding the little boy, was still moving. For more than half an hour he hung there, struggling between life and death, dying in slow agony. The guards ordered the prisoners to march past the two dead bodies and the still-struggling boy.

As Wiesel passed by, he couldn't help but turn and gaze into the boy's eyes. As he did, he heard the voice behind him ask once again, "Where is God now?"

Wiesel allowed the inner voice of his heart to answer: "Where is He? Here He is—He is hanging here on this gallows."[1]

That was a true reflection of what Wiesel believed at that moment. But God doesn't die in the midst of suffering; it only seems that way to some.

At thirty years of age, Mike Scott led a pretty good life. He was a loyal husband and father. He enjoyed hunting and fishing in remote areas of the Rocky Mountains. He had a job he liked, children he loved, and a wife he treasured.

One evening as he walked across his den to get something to eat while watching TV, he suffered a stroke that left him incapacitated. Once a robust 220 pounds, it wasn't long before he became a frail 85-pound invalid who had to be moved to a nursing home.

If anyone deserved to be bitter, to curse God, to erupt in anger and rage over the injustice of it all, it was Mike Scott. But nobody knew what he was feeling. His paralysis prevented him from talking. Those who knew him could only imagine the intense bitterness and anger that must have clouded his every thought.

One day a friend helped Mike learn to use an alphabet board to spell out sentences. Once he grasped how to use the device, he spelled out his first message. The letters came slowly, as Mike spelled out three words: "I love Jesus."[2]

In the ancient book of Job, the story's main character fell into the most tragic series of events. Four messengers came to his home, each bringing devastating reports. Job learned that he had lost his wealth—absolutely everything that he owned—and that his children had been killed. All in a single day.

Job's response is mind boggling. "Naked I came from my mother's womb, and naked I will depart. The LORD gave and the LORD has taken away; may the name of the LORD be praised."[3] Yet his ordeal was just beginning.

Job was struck with painful sores over his entire body. At this point, even his wife was adding to his misery. "Are you still holding on to your integrity? Curse God and die!"[4] Job's answer? "You are talking like a foolish woman. Shall we accept good from God, and not trouble?"[5]

Interesting question.

Suffering, as much as we dread it and try to avoid it, is a *kairos* moment. The choices we make in the midst of our suffering shape the deepest parts of our lives. Through suffering, we choose between bitterness or trust, hope or despair, love for God or hatred. Suffering is the anvil and pain is the hammer that forge the enduring shape of our lives. As the Bible records God's remarking to no one less than Satan, "Have you considered my servant Job? There is no one on earth like him."[6]

THE MEANING IN SUFFERING

I hesitate even to talk about suffering. Those of us who have felt the grip of its icy fingers have little patience for trite phrases and hollow platitudes. Shakespeare knowingly wrote, "He jests at scars who never felt a wound." In the movie *Shadowlands,* after the death of his wife, C. S. Lewis (played by Anthony Hopkins) explodes: "This is a mess! That's all anyone can say." Yes, it is. But it also is a moment unlike any other in life. Suffering takes the hardened, earthen vessels containing our lives and returns them to soft, supple clay. We will one day grow strong and firm again, but the process allows us to be changed, re-created, shaped into a new and different vessel. Due to the nature of this *kairos* moment, we must somehow see beyond the immediate pain and submit ourselves to the imprint of the Potter's hands. The new must always appear at the expense of the old.

Hear my heart. I know that urging a sufferer to look past his pain is like asking a prisoner to see his captivity as the down payment toward freedom, or like asking a woman in a windowless room to enjoy the view. Until she escapes the closed confines of her quarters, she can't see beyond the walls that conceal the outdoor panorama.

After enduring the worst year of her life, a year that brought her brother's death and her own cancer diagnosis, comedian Julia Sweeney reflected that it was as if God had looked at her well-ordered life, so neatly planned and designed, and said, "Ha!"[7]

I can sympathize with her view, but our loving God never laughs in the face of our pain. He stands right beside us, never simply looking on from a safe distance. And while He doesn't make light of our loss, God does speak to us in the midst of suffering, telling us things we might not grasp in other circumstances. If we listen carefully, we'll recognize six important benefits that come to us cloaked in pain.

To Warn Us of Danger

Sometimes God uses suffering to send us a warning that we wouldn't otherwise hear.

For years doctors and researchers wondered how leprosy—the oldest recorded human disease—produced such terrible effects. This dreaded disease produces nightmarish results: clawed hands with missing fingers, ulcerated feet, paralyzed limbs, blindness, and every conceivable kind of orthopedic defect.

It wasn't until Paul Brand began his work with leprosy patients in India that the truth became known: The disease's horrible effects come about because people with leprosy lose their ability to feel pain. The disease isn't the flesh-devouring fungus it was originally thought to be. In reality it's an illness that attacks nerve cells.

When you lose your sense of pain, you misuse your body, particularly those parts that are most dependent on pain to protect them. Someone uses a hammer with a wooden handle and gets a splinter in his hand. If he doesn't feel the splinter, he'll ignore it and get an infection. Another person steps off a curb and sprains her ankle. But since the nerve cells don't register the injury, she keeps walking, causing greater damage. Another person loses the use of the nerve that triggers the eyelids to blink every few seconds to lubricate the eyes. Without the needed moisture, his eyes dry out and he goes blind.

Without pain life becomes devastatingly vulnerable to injury. That's why Brand has written that if he could choose one gift for his leprosy patients, he would choose the gift of pain. And sometimes that is the gift God chooses for us as well.[8]

The Bible doesn't teach that every time we suffer it's because we've been sinful and disobedient to God.[9] Yet there can be little doubt that God allows some of the pain and suffering we experience to serve as an early warning system that how we are living, and the choices we are making, are terribly harmful to us. God loves us too much to isolate us from that pain, because it's the only way we can be protected from suffering even greater pain.

To Drive Us to Our Knees

A second message that God sometimes delivers through suffering is a heads-up that we've stopped depending on Him. Are you more prone to think of God when things are good or when everything seems to be going wrong? When do you look to Him with the greatest level of intensity and urgency? When are you most open and receptive to God, most willing to trust Him, and most eager to listen? Abundance can produce self-reliance, while trials tend to turn us back toward God's provision.

C. S. Lewis once called pain God's "megaphone to rouse a deaf world."[10] In personal correspondence to a friend, Lewis pursued this idea, noting that pain and suffering could even be a reflection of God's severe mercy, allowed into our lives because we wouldn't turn to Him any other way.[11] Pain as a megaphone is a terrible instrument, Lewis concedes, but it also can be our only hope.[12] Lewis himself would find this to be the case. Writing after the death of his wife, he noted that "nothing less will shake a man—or at any rate a man like me—out of his merely verbal thinking and his merely notional beliefs. He has to be knocked silly before he comes to his senses."[13]

Sadly, this is true of many of us. We have to hit bottom before we even think of looking up. But when we do, we thank God for loving us too much to shield us from the horrible ordeal that was required to raise our eyes in His direction.

In his epic tale *The Gulag Archipelago,* which recalled his imprisonment and first-hand experience of Soviet oppression, Aleksandr Solzhenitsyn reveals the power of suffering to drive us to our senses and to call us to life's deepest realizations.

> And it was only when I lay there on rotting prison straw
> that I sensed within myself the first stirrings of good.
> Gradually it was disclosed to me that the line separating
> good and evil passes not through states, nor between classes,

nor between political parties either—but right through every human heart—and through all human hearts.... So, bless you, prison, for having been in my life.[14]

To Strengthen Us

A third message we hear through times of pain is one of strength. When biologists observe this in the plant and animal world, they call it the adversity principle.

Scientists have concluded that habitual, ongoing well-being is not good for a species. In other words, an easy existence without challenge is simply not healthy. You see it in flabby zoo animals that have nothing to do but wait for their food to be delivered to them. Their muscles aren't hardened, and their senses aren't sharpened by the hunt. You see the same principle at work in rain forests. Because water is everywhere, a tree doesn't have to extend its root system more than a few feet below the surface. Then the slightest windstorm can knock it down. But a tree growing in a semiarid climate has to send its roots down thirty feet or more in search of water. Not even a gale-force wind can knock that tree down.[15]

When we look back on our times of greatest strength and deepest growth, we often see that they were preceded by a time of great pain. As Paul noted in his letter to the church at Rome, "we also rejoice in our sufferings, because we know that suffering produces perseverance; perseverance, character; and character, hope."[16]

I once heard of a legend originated in a small town in Germany that for a number of years experienced poor harvests. The townspeople prayed at the beginning of a new year saying, "God, our harvests have been so poor and so scarce, for one year will you let us plan everything?"

God said, "All right, for one year."

They immediately set their plans for abundance into motion, and God complied with their every request. Whenever they asked for rain, God sent rain. Whenever they asked for sun, God sent sun. The corn never grew higher, and the wheat had never been thicker. But when harvest came, they discovered that the tall corn had no ears, and the thick wheat had no heads of grain.

"God, you have failed us!" they cried out. "We asked for sun, and you sent sun. We asked for rain, and you sent rain. But there is no crop."

"You never asked for the harsh north winds," answered God. "Without the harsh north winds, there is no pollination, and with no pollination, there is no crop."

To Connect Us with Others

We seldom experience pain in complete isolation. Usually there is a communal aspect to suffering: the partnership of God and the involvement of fellow believers. Notice what Paul had to say in his second letter to the church at Corinth:

> [God] comes alongside us when we go through hard times, and before you know it, he brings us alongside someone else who is going through hard times so that we can be there for that person just as God was there for us.[17]

How can someone who is warm ever understand someone who is cold? How can someone who is full ever understand someone who is hungry? It's often through our own suffering that we are able to reach out to help others. As Betsie ten Boom reminded her sister Corrie just before her death in the Ravensbruck concentration camp: "[We] must tell people what we have learned here. We must tell them that there is no pit so deep that He is not deeper still. They will listen to us, Corrie, because we have been here."[18]

Mary Verghese would agree. When she was a young resident doctor, she was involved in a tragic car accident that left her disabled for life. Seeing her persistent despair, a fellow doctor simply said, "Mary, I think it's time to begin thinking of your professional future." He predicted that she would not only serve God as a physician, but that she would bring fresh qualities of sympathy and understanding to her practice.

Gradually Mary began to work with leprosy patients, hearing them whisper to themselves that the doctor in the wheelchair was more disabled than they. Their self-pity, hopelessness, and sullenness seemed to fade when Mary was around.

"At first the threads seemed so tangled and broken," she one day reflected to a fellow doctor, "but I'm beginning to think life may have a pattern after all." Mary began to see that her disability wasn't a punishment sent by God but a chance to develop her greatest asset as a doctor.

Eventually Mary learned to walk with the aid of leg braces.

She worked under scholarship in New York's Institute of Physical Medicine and Rehabilitation and ultimately headed up a new department at the Vellore, Indiana, Physiotherapy School. By turning toward God and accepting the fact that He could weave a new design for her life, Mary Verghese probably has achieved far more than she ever would have if the car accident had not occurred.[19]

To Release God's Power

What else should we listen for in the midst of suffering? A fifth message from God that comes through in times of pain is the release of His power in our lives. It often is in the eye of the storm that we see God at work most clearly. With this in mind, consider one of the most intriguing scenes from the life of Jesus:

> Walking down the street, Jesus saw a man blind from birth. His disciples asked, "Rabbi, who sinned: this man or his parents, causing him to be born blind?"
>
> Jesus said, "You're asking the wrong question. You're looking for someone to blame. There is no such cause-effect here. Look instead for what God can do."[20]

Then Jesus healed the man.

Difficult times often provide an avenue for God's power to flow into our lives. He doesn't always intervene by removing the thing that is causing us pain, though that can happen. More often we experience God's power and activity in our lives as we journey *through* the pain. The apostle Paul gave witness to this in a most personal way:

> I was given a physical condition which has been a thorn in my flesh.... Three different times I begged God to make me well again.
>
> Each time he said, "No. But I am with you; that is all you need. My power shows up best in weak people." Now I am glad to boast about how weak I am; I am glad to be a living demonstration of Christ's power, instead of showing off my own power and abilities.... [F]or when I am weak, then I am strong.[21]

One of the cardinal rules of water safety is never to swim out to a drowning person to try to help him while he is thrashing about. As long as a drowning person thinks he can help himself, he is dangerous to anyone who tries to save him. In his panic he is likely to grab the person who is trying to help and take them both down. Lifeguards know to stay just far enough away so that the person can't grab them. When the drowning person finally gives up, the rescuer makes his move. At that point, the drowning person won't work against the lifeguard. He has reached a point where he is ready to surrender and be helped.[22]

Suffering carries with it a type of forced dependence, which casts our lives before the power and presence of God. It takes away our doomed efforts to save ourselves so that we can be rescued by the One who knows exactly how to save us.

To Encourage Deeper Trust

Finally, God's message to you in the storms of pain might be an invitation to trust Him. There may never be a reason given, or even hinted at, that will explain your suffering. The only agenda is the call to radical trust, with the confidence that you are safely in the hands of God. One of the most famous proverbs reminds us to "[t]rust in the LORD with all your heart and lean not on your own understanding."[23]

A young couple lost their first child at the moment of birth. Knowing they were expecting a boy, they had chosen the name Noah and had filled his nursery with arks and animals. But he never got to sleep in the crib that stood in his joyfully prepared nursery. The parents were devastated by their baby's death.

After the funeral, during a reception at their home, the couple looked for a word, a sign, anything that would comfort them. Suddenly, on an otherwise clear summer day, a rain cloud appeared. After a brief, gentle shower, a perfectly formed rainbow arced across the sky above their home. As C. S. Lewis reminds us, "Don't you think our Lord says to you 'Peace, child, peace. Relax. Let go. Underneath are the everlasting arms. Let go, I will catch you. Do you trust me so little?'"[24]

Christian Reger spent four years as a prisoner at the Dachau concentration camp near Munich for doing nothing more than belonging to the Confessing Church, the branch of the German state church that opposed Hitler. Later, as a leader of the International Dachau Committee, Reger returned to the grounds in order to restore the camp as a monument that the world can't forget. "Nietzsche said a man can undergo torture if he knows the why of his life," Reger told author Philip Yancey. "But I, here at Dachau, learned something far greater. I learned to know the Who of my life. He was enough to sustain me then, and is enough to sustain me still."[25]

There is a make-believe story about a day when the sun did not rise. Six o'clock came and there was no sign of dawn. At seven o'clock no ray of light had yet to pierce the darkness. At noon the veil of midnight hung as a curtain. No birds sang, and only the hoot of an owl broke the silence. Then came the long hours of the afternoon, shrouded in inky black gloom.

Finally evening arrived, but no one slept. Some wept, some wrung their hands in anguish. Every church was filled with people on their knees, and there they stayed—all night, filled with terror—praying that God would save them from destruction.

After the long, seemingly endless night, millions of tear-stained faces turned toward the east. There they saw a wonderful sight. The sky began to grow red, and the sun rose high and beautiful and bright.

Suddenly everyone shouted for joy. "Thank you, God! You came to our rescue!"

They had forgotten that the sun had risen a thousand times before in their lives. One day of darkness, and the enduring faithfulness of God was instantly forgotten. All they could see was the momentary shadow of darkness. They should have remembered that God had filled their lives with thousands of sunrises, proving Himself faithful time and again.

The dark storm of suffering is never the last word. Beyond the pain is a rising sun. Or more accurately, beyond our suffering is the risen Son. Keeping our eyes fixed to the east, in faith and trust, submission and dependence, allows this *kairos* moment not only to be seized but to be formed in our lives as the Son's warmth hardens the newly shaped clay into a new form, something beautiful for God's use.

7

WHEN ASKED TO FORGIVE

Roger was given a sawed-off shotgun by a friend, and he used it.

His daughter Sarah had been riding her bike when she was hit by a drunk driver. She died almost instantly, and the driver was sent to prison for manslaughter. When he was released from prison, Roger shot him, fully intending to kill him. Charged with attempted murder, Roger was found not guilty. Despite the fact that he had deliberately tried to kill the man, the jury found the victim so repulsive that they unanimously acquitted his assailant.

Even so, it wasn't enough. The bereaved father was asked if squeezing a trigger and watching a man collapse in agony made him feel any better.

"No," he said. "Only killing him could make me feel better."

During an interview in their home, Roger's wife, Cathy, was asked how she felt. Her answer was even more chilling: "I could never be happy if Roger killed him, because that would mean that I hadn't killed him. I need to pull that trigger myself. I need to see him dead and know I'm responsible."[1]

Simon Wiesenthal, one of the best-known writers and activists for the cause of Holocaust victims, would understand the vengeance of Roger and Cathy since he himself was a victim. In his book *The Sunflower*, Wiesenthal writes about the time he was taken from a death camp to a makeshift army hospital. Once there, he was escorted by a nurse to the side of a badly wounded German soldier who had requested to have a few moments alone with a Jew. The man turned to Wiesenthal and told him how he had set an entire Jewish village on fire, burning countless numbers of men, women, and children to death. He still couldn't keep their screams from echoing through his mind. Now, near death, he wanted to seek forgiveness from someone representing the people he had killed.

After listening to the man's story and his plea for forgiveness, Wiesenthal refused.

Years later the author wondered whether he'd done the right thing. He wrote to thirty-two well-known and highly regarded scholars, social theorists, and psychologists. To each he asked, "Should I have forgiven the man on his death bed for the crime he had confessed to committing?" Twenty-six of the thirty-two told Wiesenthal that he had done the right thing in refusing to forgive the German soldier.[2]

Are you surprised to read that these highly educated and respected figures affirmed the withholding of forgiveness, or can you relate to their feelings? Bitterness, anger, resentment, hatred. Refusing to forgive and let go. This is the way of our world. It also is a way of life that creates an incredible burden, that imposes enormous bondage, and that brings with it tremendous emotional damage. What is it about the lack of forgiveness that destroys lives with such efficiency?

THE BURDEN

When you choose not to forgive, you constantly carry the pain, the bitterness, and the anger. Since you refuse to release it by forgiving the wrongdoer, you are loaded down with the burden of these damaging emotions. And it's a heavy weight to bear.

One aspect of the biblical concept of forgiveness relates to forgetfulness. In light of God's great mercy and love, David prayed, asking the Lord to "[r]emember not the sins of my youth and my rebellious ways."[3] And God gave this description of Himself through the prophet Isaiah: "I, even I, am he who blots out your transgressions, for my own sake, and remembers your sins no more."[4] On another occasion God described a time when He would make a new covenant with Israel, saying through the prophet Jeremiah: "I will forgive their wickedness and will remember their sins no more."[5]

We are to pattern our lives after God. If you fail to forgive, you fail to forget. The wrong, whether real or perceived, is kept alive. It's carried with you, day after day. Such an appendage irrevocably shapes the course of your life. Some may question whether we literally can forget the wrongs committed against us, even if we genuinely forgive the wrongdoers. God's forgetting our sins is one thing, but mere humans doing the same thing? Is that really possible? Yes, if we understand that the nature of God's forgetfulness is the choice to not hold the wrong against the wrongdoer.

If you fail to forgive the wrongs that have been committed against you, you will most certainly be unable to forget them. And with those memories, you carry around, day after day, the weight of having been wronged. It's akin to the shackles worn by those who are meant to be kept at bay. The chains bind and limit and, in the end, imprison.

No wonder Jesus gave such forceful advice when He was questioned about the extent to which we should forgive:

> Then Peter came to Jesus and asked, "Lord, how many
> times shall I forgive my brother when he sins against me?
> Up to seven times?"
>
> Jesus answered, "I tell you, not seven times, but seventy-
> seven times."[6]

Peter wanted a specific figure, a "cap" on the number of times forgiveness should be extended. But Jesus surprised Peter with His radical response: There should never be a limit on forgiveness. Your life can't bear the burden of failing to forgive.

Two unmarried sisters lived together. Because of a minor disagreement over an insignificant issue, they stopped speaking to each other. Unable to afford separate living arrangements, they continued to use the same rooms, eat at the same table—never together—and sleep in the same bedroom. All without uttering a single word to one another.

A chalk line divided their sleeping area into two halves, even to the point of separating a doorway and a fireplace. Each could come and go, cook and eat, sew and read without crossing over into the other's domain. Through the night each could hear her sister's breathing, but neither was willing to take the first step toward reconciliation. They chose to live their lives under the enormous burden that flows from failing to forgive.[7]

It's all too common to talk with people who quickly fall into a bitter description of something that happened to them years earlier. Five, ten, even twenty years past, but it's still as fresh in their hearts as if it had happened only yesterday. In terms of its effect on their lives, it might as well have happened yesterday. They keep the past wrongs alive by refusing to forgive, and the price they pay is a lack of freedom.

But it doesn't have to be that way. The burden of unforgiveness can be lifted. Clara Barton, the woman who founded the American Red Cross, learned this lesson. A friend once reminded her of an especially cruel thing that had been done to her many years before, but Barton didn't recall the incident.

Her friend prodded her, "Don't you remember it?"

"No," Barton knowingly replied, "I distinctly remember forgetting it."[8]

While Clara Barton was known for great acts of charity, Karla Faye Tucker was known as the infamous "pickax murderer." Ron

Carlson could tell you about her. He hated Tucker because she had killed his sister. He wanted to bury a pickax in her the same way she had buried one in his sister.

Then a remarkable event took place. Carlson became a Christian, and he went to prison to meet with Tucker. When he met her in the prison visitors' room, he told her he was Deborah's brother. He didn't say anything else at first.

She looked at him and asked, "You are *who?*"

He explained who he was, and she still stared, like she couldn't believe what she was hearing. Then she started to cry.

"Karla," he said, "whatever comes out of all this, I want you to know that I forgive you and that I don't hold anything against you." At that moment, Carlson recounts that all of his hatred and anger was taken away. A great weight had been taken off of his shoulders.[9]

THE BONDAGE

Failing to forgive not only saddles you with a heavy burden, it also brings bondage. It holds you captive by poisoning your emotions and then giving those damaged emotions control of your life. The wrong you suffered prevents you from moving forward with your life. It consumes you, and only forgiveness can break the cycle.

Many years ago, while in college, I spent a weekend with Tom Skinner, a well-known black evangelist who was converted to Christ when he was the leader of the largest, toughest teenage gang in New York City, the Harlem Lords. His conversion was so real that he left the gang the day after he chose to follow Christ, turning from a life of violence to a life of compassion.

He told us how a few weeks after his decision, he was playing in a football game. He made a good block on the defensive end, and his halfback scored. Suddenly the guy he blocked jumped in front of him in a rage and punched him in the stomach. Next he hacked him across the back. When Skinner fell, the boy viciously kicked him, shouting, "You dirty black n——! I'll teach you a thing or two!"

The old Tom Skinner would have jumped up and killed his opponent. Literally. Instead the power and presence of Christ took over, and this new believer chose a different path. He stood up, looked the boy in the face, and said, "You know, because of Jesus Christ I love you anyway." Then Skinner went back to the game.

When the contest was over, the boy who had attacked him came over and said, "Tom, I'm sorry. Tell me more about your Christ."

Such is the power of forgiveness to break the chains of bondage. The forgiveness of Christ freed Tom Skinner from a life of crime and violence. And in turn it broke through the hatred and bigotry of an opponent on the football field. Forgiveness breaks down strongholds even when they bind an entire nation.

South Africa was ruled after its independence from Britain in 1931 under a system known as apartheid, meaning "apartness" in Afrikaans. It was a system designed to perpetuate the privileges and political power of the white minority on the grounds that black

South Africans were not capable of self-rule. Under apartheid, blacks couldn't travel on whites-only buses, couldn't picnic on whites-only beaches, and couldn't take their sick children to whites-only hospitals.

For eighteen years in a prison on the shores of Robben Island, cell block B housed a black antiapartheid activist named Nelson Mandela. While behind bars, Mandela became a Christian after watching a Billy Graham crusade on television. Set free in 1990, he resumed political life and was elected president of South Africa. He went from powerless prisoner to the most powerful office in the land within four years. What led to such an unbelievable turn of events? The former Anglican archbishop of Cape Town, Desmond Tutu, explained it well, saying, "Had Nelson Mandela...not been willing to forgive, we would not have even reached first base."[10]

THE BROKENNESS

Finally, when there is no forgiveness, there is relational brokenness. The bitterness that relentlessly grows from a failure to forgive seeps out like a poison that begins to slowly destroy your entire relational world.

Have you ever been in a canyon or a cave where the sound of your voice creates an echo? Whatever words you cry out come back to you over and over again. The failure to forgive resounds throughout our lives in just such a way. I recall reading once of a teacher who asked her students to write down, in thirty seconds, the names of all the people they disliked. Some students could think of only one name during the half-minute. Others listed as many as fourteen. The interesting fact that emerged from the research was that those who disliked the most people were themselves the most widely disliked.[11]

That's not news if you read the Scriptures. "Do not judge, or you too will be judged," the Bible reminds us. "For in the same way you judge others, you will be judged, and with the measure you use, it will be measured to you."[12] The relational brokenness goes further, for the Bible also says, "if you forgive men when they sin against you, your heavenly Father will also forgive you. But if you do not forgive men their sins, your Father will not forgive your sins."[13] There is reciprocity. The granting of forgiveness leads to the receiving of forgiveness. And it's not just with other people, but with God as well. If you don't forgive others, you won't experience the healing touch of forgiveness in your own life.

That may seem unfair, but doesn't it make sense that untended brokenness would lead to more brokenness? And this is a brokenness that no one can endure for long, for our heart's cry will always move us toward the hope of absolution.

In one of Ernest Hemingway's stories, a Spanish father decides to reconcile with his son who had run away to Madrid. The father takes out an ad in the *El Liberal* newspaper: "PACO MEET ME AT HOTEL MONTANA NOON TUESDAY ALL IS FORGIVEN PAPA." Paco is a common name in Spain, and when the father goes to the square, he finds eight hundred young men waiting—and hoping—that their fathers will be there to welcome them.[14]

We're all like those Pacos: desperate for forgiveness, empty without it. But as long as our lives are shaped by the burden, bondage, and brokenness of unforgiveness, we'll never know the freedom that comes with forgiveness. There is a way, however, to break the bonds of an unforgiving spirit. That is the beauty of this *kairos* moment.

A BETTER CHOICE

Linguistics professor Deborah Tannen has written that we live in an "argument culture" that "urges us to approach the world—and the people in it—in an adversarial frame of mind." This culture rests on the assumption that "opposition is the best way to get anything done."

Tannen's verdict? Not true.[15] The Bible's verdict? Ditto.

When we choose forgiveness, we enjoy the freedom that comes with it. Bitterness and resentment are released, and relational health is restored with other people and with God. That's the strategic importance of the decision to forgive. It's a *kairos* moment that will bless our lives through the rest of our days.

With so much to gain and only negative emotions to lose, why is forgiveness so difficult? C. S. Lewis brought this dilemma to light when he commented that everybody thinks forgiveness is a lovely idea until they have something to forgive.[16] Or as Philip Yancey concedes, "forgiveness is an unnatural act."[17]

"I went around saying for a long time that I am not one of

those Christians who is heavily into forgiveness—that I am one of the other kind," confessed author Anne Lamott. "By the time I decided to become one of the ones who *is* heavily into forgiveness, it was like trying to become a marathon runner in middle age."[18]

Yet there is a way to succeed in doing just that.

It was just over one hundred years ago, in Pike County, Kentucky, that a jury sentenced eight people to life in prison and ordered a ninth defendant to be hanged for the slaying of four people. All nine carried the name Hatfield. The four murder victims all were McCoys.

Most of us have heard about the famous feud between these two clans. It's part of American folklore. The Hatfields, living mainly on the Virginia side of the Big Sandy River, and the McCoys, living in Pike County, Kentucky, fought on and off for a dozen years. Historians aren't sure, but many estimate that before it ended, up to twenty people died in that bloody little war.

Some say the feud started in 1878 over a McCoy pig that ended up in a Hatfield pen. Others say the dispute stemmed from the Civil War, in which the Hatfields fought for the Confederacy and the McCoys for the Union. Romantics say the feud began over the secret love affair of Johnse Hatfield and Roseanna McCoy, who eventually bore him a child out of wedlock.

Whatever the cause, violence erupted in August 1882 when a member of the Hatfield clan was stabbed two dozen times and then shot in Pike County. The Hatfields then kidnapped three McCoys and killed them all. The bitter conflict escalated until it reached its peak on New Year's Day in 1888, when the

Hatfields attacked the McCoy home on the Blackberry Fork of Pond Creek in Pike County, burning it to the ground and killing two children.

That's the bloody history of these two families. Yet in the spring of 2000, the descendents of the feuding parties got together for a picnic that included no greater contest than a softball game. All it took was a single member of one of the families deciding it was time to reconcile.

What allows forgiveness to become a choice that shifts the surging current of broken relationships, hard feelings, bitterness, and resentment? How do you seize the *kairos* nature of forgiveness and make it a moment that changes the course of the remainder of your life? It's not done quickly, or easily. Taking advantage of this life-defining moment requires attention and commitment.

WARMING UP FOR FORGIVENESS

When it comes to forgiving someone, the Bible gives five specific steps. But before we investigate the process of forgiveness, we need to look at three important warm-up exercises. The workout of forgiveness demands a well-prepared soul.

First, you have to admit the need to forgive. Some people deny that there's a problem. They disavow any bitterness, resentment, or anger toward the other person. Or they acknowledge the divide but deny that it's an issue of any significance. The *kairos* nature of forgiveness can't be seized until you realize you *need* to forgive.

Second, you have to accept the responsibility to forgive. You may not be responsible for what another person did, but you are responsible for how you *react* to what he did, and that includes the responsibility to forgive. "Be gentle with one another, sensitive," the apostle Paul instructs. "Forgive one another as quickly and thoroughly as God in Christ forgave you."[19] Paul even added the instruction to "never hold grudges. Remember, the Lord forgave you, so you must forgive others."[20] Forgiveness is not a gift to the one who wronged you, nor is it a denial of the pain that was inflicted. Instead it's a personal responsibility you carry as a mandate from God independent of all other considerations.

Third, ask God for help. Before you rush into the challenge of forgiveness, invite God into the process. Ask Him to give you a tender heart, strength you don't have, and the steadfastness to walk through the entire process without bailing out along the way.

FIVE STEPS OF FORGIVENESS

Once you've admitted the need, accepted the responsibility, and asked God for help, then you're ready to walk through the five steps that lead to truly forgiving someone.[21] As you work through these steps, remember that forgiveness is a process. It's not like a light switch that you simply flip off or on. It's more realistic to think of the steps of forgiveness as a road map to follow in reaching a destination. It might take awhile to get there, but you can know that you're heading in the right direction.

Step One: Restore the Attitude of Love

Before the process of forgiveness can begin, you first must restore the attitude of love. I don't mean working yourself up into a phony emotional state. What I mean is that you try to see the other person the way God sees her, with compassion and grace. No matter what she's done, she matters to God. In His economy, she is a person of inexpressible value and worth. This is why the Bible reminds us:

> If anyone boasts, "I love God," and goes right on hating his
> brother or sister, thinking nothing of it, he is a liar. If he
> won't love the person he can see, how can he love the God
> he can't see? The command we have from Christ is blunt:
> Loving God includes loving people. You've got to love both.[22]

Dietrich Bonhoeffer reflects that we must meet others "as the person that he already is in Christ's eyes.... Spiritual love recognizes the true image of the other person which he has received from Jesus Christ; the image that Jesus Christ himself embodied and would stamp upon all men.[23]

Seeing others through the eyes of Christ, even when we feel no warmth of compassion toward that person, is crucial. In those instances, we shouldn't worry ourselves with whether we love someone—we simply should act as if we do. When we act as if we love our neighbors, then we slowly but surely begin to *really* love them.

The *Star Wars* movies present a world-view that often is far from Christian. But at other times, it seems as though the script is taken directly from the pages of Christian theology. One such parallel appears in the second trilogy when Luke Skywalker is being seduced by the dark side of "the force." The evil lord tells Luke to give in to his hate, for when he does, then he will have crossed over into the dark side. Those words are true. If you injure or strike out at those you hate, you'll find yourself hating them more, because you're giving in to the hate.

If loving your "enemy" seems beyond you, remember that you've actually been exercising that type of love for quite some time. You know someone who has caused you great pain through countless mistakes and failures. This same person has hurt a great many other people over the years and has done things that deserve enormous judgment. Yet somehow, time and again, you've been able to separate those actions from who the person really is. You've been able to offer some level of forgiveness to this person, despite the bulk of his actions.

That person, of course, is you.[24]

Step Two: Release the Past

Once you've restored the attitude of love, you're ready for the next step. It's time to release the past.

Bible teacher John Haggai tells a story about a woman whom all the kids he grew up with called Aunt Edith. She came home one day and found all five of her children huddled around something of great interest. As she got closer, she saw to her horror that they were playing with five baby skunks!

At the top of her voice, she screamed, "Children, *run!*" And they all did. Each one grabbed a skunk and ran![25]

Not exactly what Aunt Edith had in mind. Nor is it what God had in mind in relation to releasing the past through the act of forgiveness. True forgiveness can only be based on the present, not the past. It has to do with who you're going to be, not what might have gone before.

The Bible tells us that "[a] man's wisdom gives him patience; it is to his glory to overlook an offense."[26] To overlook something literally means a deliberate effort to avert the eyes, to make the conscious decision not to fix your gaze. Our tendency is just the opposite. We want to hover over the offenses committed against us. We build up the insult in our minds instead of turning our mind's eye in another direction. And in truth, most offenses deserve this release, for as C. S. Lewis wrote in correspondence to a friend, "one has to remember that when people 'hurt' [you]…in 99 cases out of 100 they intended to hurt very much less, or not at all, and are often quite unconscious of the whole thing." Lewis adds, "I've learned this from the cases in which I was the 'hurter.' "[27] He adds another helpful word, namely, "We are *all* fallen creatures and *all* very hard to live with."[28]

Step Three: Reconstruct the Relationship

The third step toward true forgiveness involves reconstructing the broken relationship. Here is the real labor of forgiveness. We want the act of forgiving to be internal, something kept completely private. But that's not the way forgiveness works. It's not simply a matter of what you have determined within yourself, it's also what is settled between you and the forgiven party. And the teaching of Christ is clear; it doesn't matter whether you are the offending party or the one who has been offended. It still is up to you to take the initiative.

In Matthew 5, Jesus speaks to the one who was the offender:

Therefore, if you are offering your gift at the altar and there remember that your brother has something against you, leave your gift there in front of the altar. First go and be reconciled to your brother; then come and offer your gift.[29]

And in Matthew 18, Jesus speaks to the one who has been offended:

If your brother sins against you, go and show him his fault, just between the two of you.[30]

In either situation three steps can be found that reconstruct the relationship.

First, Jesus says that we are to stop whatever we're doing, even if it means leaving a gift at the altar. There is something that needs to be addressed in a tangible, interpersonal manner.

Second, with very few exceptions, we are to go to the person from whom we are estranged.[31] No third party will do, nor must we fall into the trap of saying that it's the other person's responsibility. "This business of forgiving is by no means a simple thing," writes Helmut Thielicke, a German theologian who lived through the horrors of Nazism. "We make of forgiveness a law of reciprocity. And this never works. For then both of us say to ourselves, "The other fellow has to make the first move."[32]

Now let's be honest. Making the first move to be reconciled with another is the *last* thing we want to do. It's messy, uncomfortable, and awkward. "We tend to relate to one another with the hidden purpose of maintaining our comfort," notes psychologist and author Larry Crabb, "and avoiding whatever sort of interaction we find threatening."[33] So here's what we'd *rather* do: We'd prefer to go through six friends and four acquaintances telling *them* all about our problem, painting the other person as an awful creature with ourselves as the innocent victim. We'll feel better because we've gotten it off of our chest, but we won't ever bother to confront the person.

The only healthy way to resolve this problem is to go immediately and directly to the person with whom the relationship is broken. The longer you wait, the more bitter you will become, and the deeper the conflict will descend. A relational break is like a wound. If it isn't attended to quickly, it will become infected and grow far worse than it ever was in the beginning. Though a radical step, treatment can only begin by going directly to the person at the very onset of the conflict.

After you have stopped what you are doing and have gone to the person, Jesus prescribes a third action: Be reconciled.

When face to face with someone we need to forgive, our natural desire will be to tell him what a terrible person he is, how angry we have been with him, and how right it has been for us to have been so angry.

However, justifying our anger isn't reconciliation, it's attacking, it's accusation, it's picking a fight. Reconciliation is apologizing for wrongs *you* have done, even if the wrong is a failure to forgive, and seeking to be made right with the other person. It's admitting how your actions or reactions have contributed to the broken relationship. It's taking time to listen in order to understand the other person's feelings, perspectives, and motivations. It's truth telling, transparency, vulnerability, and the commitment to restoring community. It's going with a spirit that seeks above all else to be reconciled.

And that's a tough assignment. Let's not sugarcoat it. That's why I said this is the real work of forgiveness.

Step Four: Reopen the Future

The fourth major step of forgiveness is to reopen the future, and this can't be conditional. There will be no guarantees that you'll never be hurt again. Chances are, you will. Forgiveness is less about expectations than it is about acceptance. Jesus addressed this head-on.

> If you see your friend going wrong, correct him. If he responds, forgive him. Even if it's personal against you and repeated seven times through the day, and seven times he says, "I'm sorry, I won't do it again," forgive him.[34]

Does this mean that you become a doormat or that you constantly put yourself in a place where others can target you for abuse? No. Granting forgiveness and volunteering for more abuse are two very different things.

Does it mean you have to pretend that the actions of the offending party weren't wrong or even evil? Does it mean that you find the person who deeply hurt you to suddenly be a person you want to spend a lot of time with? No. Someone might rob my home, and I could forgive him for doing it. But that doesn't mean he shouldn't go to jail.

Forgiveness simply means choosing to let go of all that seeks to attach itself to our offenses. This is behind the meaning of the word. *Forgive* literally means to "give something up." If we are going to reopen the future, and really forgive, we must not brood over the wrong that was done, letting bitterness seep in and rule the day. Instead we turn loose the memory of the hurt so we can embrace the healing.

Step Five: Reaffirm the Relationship

The final step in true and complete forgiveness, the kind that enables us to seize the life-defining moment it offers, is to reaffirm the relationship. If forgiveness doesn't end in celebration, then it hasn't occurred. "I can forgive, but I'll never forget" is like saying "I can overlook a wrong done, but not the one who wronged me." Yet forgiveness, if it's anything, speaks to the person behind the offense, not simply the offense itself.

A Chance Meeting

"A ticket to Haarlem, please." My Dutch wasn't very good, but the person behind the window in the Amsterdam train station understood the name of the city, and soon I was on my way to the house of the ten Boom family. I was unashamedly on a pilgrimage.

In the late 1930s Corrie ten Boom was a middle-aged woman living in a small town in the Netherlands. Horrified by the German onslaught against the Jewish people of her country, Corrie and her family began to hide those most threatened. Today you can tour her home and see the wall behind which so many Jewish persons were hidden, protected from capture and, most certainly, death.

The actions of the ten Boom family were discovered, and they were arrested. Corrie was sent first to a prison in Vught built by German occupying forces for political prisoners. Soon she was transported deep within Germany to a place whose very name struck terror, Ravensbruck, the notorious women's extermination camp.

Her father died within the first two weeks of his arrest. Corrie and her sister Betsie lasted through Vught and then Ravensbruck, where Betsie eventually died. But Corrie survived the humiliation, the beatings, the deprivation, the starvation, the sickness, the stench. Released on a clerical error a week before she was scheduled to enter the ovens, Corrie spent the rest of her life speaking of Christ's love, forgiveness, mercy, and sustenance wherever she went. Eventually her story was captured in the best-selling book *The Hiding Place,* one of the most stirring books you'll ever read.

Corrie ten Boom became an ambassador to the world.

It was years later, at a church service in Munich, that she saw him. He was a balding, heavyset man in a gray overcoat, but she remembered him in a different guise. He was the SS man who had stood guard at the shower room door in the processing center at Ravensbruck. She saw him as she had seen him years before: in a blue uniform and visored cap, holding a leather riding crop. She had been forced to walk naked past this cruel, leering man. Throughout the years following the war, this was the first Nazi jailer that she'd seen. Suddenly it all returned. The roomful of mocking men, the heaps of clothing, her sister's pain-blanched face.

The former SS officer came up to her immediately.

"How grateful I am for your message, *Fräulein*," he said. "To think that, as you say, He has washed my sins away!" Then he stretched forth his hand to shake hers and told her what she already knew.

"I was a guard at Ravensbruck. I have become a Christian. I know that God has forgiven me for the cruel things that I did there, but I would like to hear it from your lips as well. *Fräulein*, will you forgive me?"

Corrie thought this would be impossible. Her sister had died in that notorious concentration camp. It was too much to erase, too much to forgive, too much to ask. She who had spoken so often to so many about the need to forgive kept her hand at her side.

Undaunted, the man's hand remained outstretched. She just

looked at it. But she knew that forgiveness was not an act of emotion, but an act of the will. It was a decision. It was a *kairos* moment that would echo throughout her life.

Suddenly she thought, "Jesus died for this man; am I going to ask for more?" So she prayed, "Lord Jesus, forgive me and help me to forgive him." She tried to smile; she struggled to raise her hand but could not. She felt nothing, not the slightest spark of warmth or charity.

Again she prayed: "Lord Jesus, I cannot forgive him. Give me Your forgiveness."

She took the hand of her former captor. And when she did, the most extraordinary thing happened. From her shoulder, along her arm and through her hand, a current seemed to pass from her to him, while into her heart flowed an overwhelming love for this formerly evil figure.[35]

That same love can flow into your heart too.

8

WHEN EXPERIENCING TEMPTATION

He began early in life, doing what many young boys do—sneaking up to his uncle's room to drool through old copies of *Playboy*. Years later he and his fiancée did their share of sexual experimentation before they got married. But his dalliances with lust didn't rise up and stare him in the face until he was on a business trip in Rochester, New York. The photo of an exotic dancer—a former Miss Peach Bowl, in fact—seemed to jump out of the newspaper. She looked fresh and inviting; the enchanting kind of Southern girl you'd see on TV commercials for fried chicken. Only this one had no clothes on.

Rationalizations came readily to mind. To be an effective Christian, he needed to experience all of life, right? Didn't Jesus hang around with prostitutes and other types of sinners? All he had to do, he told himself, was to make sure that when he looked at Miss Peach Bowl, he didn't start to imagine having intercourse with her. That way he wouldn't be committing adultery in his heart.

Encouraged by such thoughts, he quickly hailed a taxi and was on his way.

Miss Peach Bowl was everything the ad promised. She danced superbly and was even something of an acrobat. She began her act fully dressed, then teased the room full of men until she wore almost nothing. The stage was encircled by whooping, leering men who stuffed folded bills under what was left of her clothing. Then she cartwheeled across the stage and was gone.

The man walked out with a strange sensation. No one from home had seen him. There didn't seem to be any harm done. In one sense, nothing had changed. In the deepest of senses, however, *everything* had changed. He'd been tempted to enter the room of the deadly sin of lust, and he'd gladly accepted the invitation. And that solitary decision began a downward descent that eventually cost him everything, including his marriage, his children, and his career.[1]

This is the crux of a story that was told in an anonymously written article for *Leadership Journal,* aptly titled "The War Within," and it's a war we all must wage, for there is no natural end to sin. Sin is not an isolated event that can be controlled. It's a cancer that, if not stopped, will destroy your life. That's what makes facing temptation a life-defining *kairos* moment.

In many Christian circles, our attention is directed toward sinful acts instead of the temptation that precedes the act. Temptation, we are reminded, is not a sin. Jesus Himself was tempted and resisted, so we choose to focus instead on the sinful activities themselves. This view is doing great harm, and it's time to clear things up.

Yes, Jesus was tempted. No, temptation is not a sin. But dismissing temptation as unimportant is simply naive. The *kairos* moment, when everything is on the line, comes *at the time of temptation*. It's the choice you make at *that* moment that is life-determining. The apostle James writes of the pivotal role of temptation, noting that "after desire has conceived, it gives birth to sin; and sin, when it is full-grown, gives birth to death."[2] Temptation is the first step into hell's clutches.

OUR CRAFTY ENEMY

Every person is tempted. Not just on an occasional basis, but repeatedly, every day, many times a day. Temptations jump onto our pathways, enter into our minds, flit across our vision, and brush over our hands with untiring repetition.

But that's not all. The temptations often are custom-designed and custom-timed from the Evil One himself. They are diabolic and sinister. The enemy is well aware of your weaknesses, contemplates the perfect times to strike, and plots when you are at your most vulnerable.[3]

Satan is a specialist in your personal and spiritual ruin. That's why Peter warned a group of Christians about Satan using these sobering words: "Be self-controlled and alert. Your enemy the devil prowls around like a roaring lion looking for someone to devour."[4] A lion stalks its prey, studies its victim, and analyzes every angle, biding its time for the perfect moment to pounce. And there is no dimension to our life that is impregnable, no matter who we are.

Gordon MacDonald was the senior minister at a large New England church before becoming the president of Inter-Varsity Christian Fellowship. Along the way he wrote numerous best-selling Christian books. He was asked to give a speech at a college commencement, and before the festivities began he spent time with a member of the school's board in the president's office. They were talking and getting better acquainted when suddenly the board member raised a provocative question that stood out to MacDonald—and would for years to come: "If Satan were to blow you out of the water, how do you think he would do it?"

"I'm not sure I know," MacDonald answered. "All sorts of ways, I suppose; but I know there's one way he wouldn't get me. He'd never get me in the area of my personal relationships. That's one place where I have no doubt that I'm as strong as you can get."

It wasn't long after that conversation that MacDonald's world broke open, and in the area of the most important personal relationship he stewarded. He betrayed the covenants of his marriage and became, in his own words, a "broken-world person." When we don't think we are susceptible in a given area, we let down our guard and become more exposed than ever. MacDonald's reflections on his descent into temptation's lair are penetrating: "A chain of seemingly innocent choices became destructive, and it was my fault. Choice by choice by choice, each easier to make, each becoming gradually darker. And then my world broke—in the very area I had predicted I was safe."[5]

The Path into Sin

If temptation is unavoidable, and if Satan custom designs temptations to have a greater chance of snaring us, what can we do to resist? A first step is to recognize the seemingly harmless choices that ultimately can lead us into darkness. Falling into sin usually isn't a bold decision to forsake a righteous life in exchange for a carnal one. Instead it takes the form of an unwise choice that leads to a series of even more foolish choices. There is a progressive nature to the process. What begins as a seemingly innocent matter can lead us to the pit.

How then can we be wise at the very beginning and make the choices that will protect our lives? Success involves recognizing the four phases that temptation takes us through. And it all begins with a simple look.

We Look

In the earliest stages of temptation, sin is never repulsive. On the contrary, it is attractive, even alluring. No wonder temptation often begins with the invitation to simply look its way. But looks can be and often are deceiving.

I once read about a police officer who was sent out in an ice storm to keep people away from a fallen power line. As he stood watch, the power line was carrying a current that shot sparks through the limbs of a tree. The sparks reflected off the ice on the branches, sending out a rainbow of glimmering colors. "How could anything so beautiful," he thought, "be so deadly?"[6]

Because of temptation's allure, if we're not careful we won't avert our glance. We'll stare, letting its image soak into our minds and hearts through the window of our eyes, allowing its vision to wrap itself around our weaknesses and sinful desires. This is why the apostle Peter, when discussing a group of people who had given themselves over to sin, made the telling observation that "[w]ith eyes full of adultery, they...have left the straight way and wandered off."[7]

But what does it mean to turn our gaze in temptation's direction? Let's say the temptation is sexual.[8] To look temptation's way would not simply be to glance in its direction. If I'm walking down the street and a scantily clad young woman suddenly walks into my view, it's impossible not to observe her and to have my thoughts turn almost instantly to a physical appreciation of her appearance.

So what does it mean to look at her in such a way that I've taken the first step toward giving in to temptation? Simply put, it would be if I looked at her with *lust*. This isn't the simple appreciation of a woman's beauty or even being sexually aroused by a member of the opposite sex. You were made to be attracted to beauty and to find certain things sexually appealing. But lust takes this a step further. It's the playing out of those temptations within the theater of your mind. When Jesus taught that to look at a woman with a lustful eye was adulterous, He was referring to the look that was an ongoing habit, focused on a single person in light of a mental fantasy.[9] When we do this, we have turned our eyes toward temptation.

We Explore

The second phase, after we have turned temptation's way to take a lingering look, is that of exploration. With the actual sinful act still light-years away, we investigate issues related to what would be *involved* with the act, which, of course, we are sure we'll never actually pursue.

This is the stage in which we first make rationalizations to justify our anticipated behavior. At least I do. We haven't actually done anything; we're just working things through in our mind out of simple curiosity. This is also the time when God comes to us, in the midst of our temptation, and delivers a swift kick to the hind-quarters of our conscience. The Bible tells us:

> No temptation has seized you except what is common to
> man. And God is faithful; he will not let you be tempted
> beyond what you can bear. But when you are tempted,
> he will also provide a way out so that you can stand up
> under it.[10]

As we've seen, temptation is inevitable. But giving in to every single satanic intrigue because we feel we're helpless to resist is not. We are commanded to stand up to temptation, and we are promised that God will meet our efforts at resistance with His supernatural support.[11]

We Seek

We can stop temptation at the first phase, by looking away and redirecting our thinking after we first are confronted with temptation. Failing that, we can end it by refusing to devote any mental energy to considering what it would be like if we were to actually pursue the thing we looked at and found so appealing. But if we fail to stop at either of the first two phases, the inevitable third step is taken. We go in search of the sin, placing ourselves within close proximity. It's as if we position ourselves in such a way that if the sin should come along, we'll at least be in the neighborhood. We haven't actually committed the act, but all the necessary arrangements have been made.

Consider how this could play out. You're committed to your marriage, and you've never questioned your mate's love. But you see someone attractive at work, and you give her more than a passing glance. You let your eyes connect, and you allow your mind to wander. Just a bit. Hey, she's pretty and you're a normal guy. Nothing wrong with admiring a member of the opposite sex.

Soon you're much more aware of this woman. You glance around to see if she's in the company cafeteria. You find out her name—just a quick check of the company directory. You ask others about her—casually, of course. At meetings you watch where she sits and position yourself accordingly. It's not long before you have a chance to strike up a conversation.

Lunch follows. Maybe even with two or three other colleagues. You send a little message on e-mail. She replies. You think of something funny to send her way, and the relationship begins.

Soon you're having lunch together without the colleagues, and business matters never even make the agenda. You talk about your marriage, cautiously at first, but eventually you admit that there are some real deficiencies in that area. She hands you something from across the table, and you let your hand pass gently over hers. The degree to which you confide in each other increases, and the friendship is allowed to develop unchecked into something more. Much more.

We Act

So far, nothing physical has happened that could be classified as adultery. You've looked, you've arranged to meet the person, you've had lunch and intimate conversations. But unless you cut it off right now, the next and final step is soon to follow. You'll act on the temptation. And when you do, you shouldn't be surprised. For quite some time you were drawing ever closer to the flame.

No greater case study exists for the downward slide that temptation brings than the fall of King David, one of the greatest lovers of God who ever lived.[12] First, temptation came his way. A beautiful woman decided to bathe on a rooftop, exposed to the view of others. And she *was* beautiful. The Bible even makes use of a rare phrase denoting exceptional beauty, a term reserved for people of striking physical appearance. David noticed the woman, but he did more than simply glance and then immediately look away. He allowed his glance to turn into a long, lingering, lustful stare.

Then he explored the sin by sending someone to find out

about this extraordinary woman. All he asked about was her name, nothing more. Just an innocent inquiry.

The servant whom David sent came back with the information but delivered it in an intriguing fashion. In that day, when you gave someone's name, you would say something like "David son of Jesse" or "Tamar daughter of David." The custom was to speak in terms of lineage. Yet David's servant, perhaps sensing more than a passing interest on the king's part, gave the following reply: "Isn't this Bathsheba, the daughter of Eliam and the wife of Uriah the Hittite?"[13]

Translation to the king: "This is a married woman."

Here was the perfect chance for David to come to his senses. He could interrupt his slide into temptation's clutching grasp. The servant had lit up the exit sign. The warning had been sounded.

But David didn't take heed. Instead he went straight to temptation's third phase and sought Bathsheba out, even sending someone to go and get her. He deliberately put himself in a position where the actual sin could take place. His mind could have been racing with rationalizations: "I only want to get to know her better. Nothing wrong with just saying hello. I'm not going to actually do anything."

Then he went ahead with phase four. He acted. As J. Allan Petersen has noted, David "could not see beyond the moment." Petersen, who has reflected extensively on the issue of marital infidelity, adds that David modeled how "temptation appeals to desire, desire creates the fantasy, fantasy sparks the feeling, and the feelings cry out for the act."[14] The progressive nature of sin's enticement can't be denied.

David, of course, reaped the consequences. It not only cost him the completion of God's plan for his life, it cost him the very life of his son. He didn't see the *kairos* nature of that first glimpse of Bathsheba's bathing on the roof. This is Satan's great scheme, to try to blind us to the progression of temptation. As C. S. Lewis's fictional demon Screwtape advises his young nephew, Wormwood, in the fine art of tempting a human: "Let an insult or a woman's body so fix his attention outward that he does not reflect 'I am now entering into the state called Anger—or the state called Lust.'"[15] Anything but seeing the life-defining nature of the moment.

How to Resist Temptation

Dag Hammarskjold, former secretary general of the United Nations, noted, "You cannot play with the animal in you without becoming wholly animal, play with falsehood without forfeiting your right to truth, play with cruelty without losing your sensitivity of mind. He who wants to keep his garden tidy doesn't reserve a plot for weeds."[16] This is the key to resisting temptation: We must refuse to give it a foothold. We must resist its efforts to place us under its spell at the very earliest of introductions. "All alone," Petersen writes, "[temptation] is utterly powerless. To succeed, temptation always needs a partner—someone to agree with it, to dance with it, to open the door for it, to welcome it in."[17]

To add to the danger, as we allow ourselves to descend the staircase of temptation, giving in at each successive level, we will find ourselves increasingly desensitized. Each entry into the successive stages of temptation is like a dose of novocaine in our spiritual system. We grow numb to the significance and consequences of our choices. The more we follow temptation's lead, the more callous we become. "And thus gradually the malignant foe enters fully," wrote Thomas à Kempis, "since he was not resisted at first. And the longer one is careless about resisting, so much the weaker is he every day, and the foe more powerful against him."[18]

If temptation is this strong and this deceptive, how can we resist it? As children of God, we have four resources available to us that will keep temptation from turning into sin.

Depend on God's Truth

The first resource to draw from is the example set by Jesus. When Christ was tempted, what did *He* do? Here's a clue, and it worked against every line of Satan's attack: "It is written… It is written… It is written…"

Jesus resisted temptation through a dependence on the truth and reality of the Word of His Father. This approach penetrated the life and thoughts of the apostle Paul, leading him to remind his young apprentice, Timothy:

> All Scripture is inspired by God and is useful to teach us
> what is true and to make us realize what is wrong in our
> lives. It straightens us out and teaches us to do what is right.
> It is God's way of preparing us in every way, fully equipped
> for every good thing God wants us to do.[19]

Scripture dispels all rationalizations. It obliterates the excuses we are tempted to believe as we progress merrily along the path of self-destruction. It illumines the right path and the correct course of action.

To resist temptation, we must have a deep and penetrating knowledge of God's precepts for life. They must not be held loosely or in disregard. They should stand in the vanguard of our journey. Nothing in our situation can be allowed to loosen their hold on our lives or weaken their power in showing us how life is to be lived. The Bible is the mirror into which we look to see if what we are doing is what we should be doing. The first line of defense against sin is knowledge, understanding what is right and wrong, true and false, good and evil.

Refuse to Go Along

Second, we must simply refuse to cooperate. We aren't powerless against temptation. The devil can't *make* us do anything. That's why the Bible encourages us to "[y]ell a loud *no* to the Devil."[20]

One of President Ronald Reagan's aides visited the largest high school in the Bronx. He spoke for forty-five minutes to more than three thousand young people, urging them to say no to drugs. At the end of his speech, he said he needed a volunteer. He selected a young man who appeared to be a senior and brought him up front.

"Now, young man, what I would like for you to do is take off all your clothes in front of these students."

"No way!" the boy said. "I'm not going to do that."

"You've forgotten who I am," the man continued. "I'm an aide to the president of the United States. I'm very close to him. I could get on the phone right now and have him command you to take off all your clothes."

"You can get the president to call," the boy replied, "but I'm not going to do that in front of these guys."

"Oh," the aide said, "I understand what you want. You want money." He took out his wallet and handed the student a twenty-dollar bill. "Now, for this twenty dollars, would you take off your clothes?"

"No!" the boy insisted. "You could hand me a hundred-dollar bill, but I'm not going to do it!"

The speaker then turned to the auditorium packed with the boy's peers and said, "Would you like to see him take his clothes off?"

The kids began chanting, "Yeah! Yeah! Take your clothes off! Take your clothes off!"

"They can go on all day long," the boy said. "I'm not going to do it."

Then the speaker made his point. "I want you to understand what you've just done. You've said no to something stupid. You've said no to power. You've said no to money. And you've said no to your peers. If you can say no in here, you can do it out there. Go say no to drugs."

The same principle is true for any temptation that comes our way. As a determined act of the will, we can just say no.

Run Away

A third resource at our disposal may seem insultingly unsophisticated, but then all the shields against temptation's arrows are elementary in nature. When temptation rears its head, simply *run away*. You must learn how to quickly remove yourself from the danger zone.

Just ask Joseph. As a young man—perhaps as young as seventeen, but certainly not out of his twenties—he was confronted with a major temptation that coincided with a vulnerable period in his life.

> Now Joseph was well-built and handsome, and after a while his master's wife took notice of Joseph and said, "Come to bed with me!"
>
> But he refused.... "How then could I do such a wicked thing and sin against God?" And though she spoke to Joseph day after day, he refused to go to bed with her or even be with her.
>
> One day he went into the house to attend to his duties, and none of the household servants was inside. She caught him by his cloak and said, "Come to bed with me!" But he left his cloak in her hand and ran out of the house.[21]

We can all learn needed lessons from Joseph: If she's attractive to you, back off. If he's instrumental in leading you down a path that dishonors God, end the relationship. If I begin saying things that are innocent on the surface, but I know there is another message behind it, I need to shut up. If you can't seem to stay away from downloading pornography off the Internet, move the computer into a more public area or simply get off the Net, keeping e-mail and using the Web, only when necessary, at the library.

The bottom line is to remove yourself from temptation's playground. This is why the apostle Paul, when giving instructions on battling temptation, simply said to *flee*.[22] In fact, his directions were so explicit that a direct translation from the Greek reads more along the lines of "make it your habit to flee!"[23] This is a call to be on the alert constantly. You can't stand toe-to-toe with temptation, go fifteen rounds, and win. You must remove yourself and run away as fast and as far as you can.

Seek Out Accountability

Posted throughout a college campus near my home are signs reading "Don't run alone." The obvious intent is to warn students of the dangers of jogging around campus by themselves. There is obvious safety in numbers. It's no different in regard to our walk with Christ and the danger of sin. We need to take advantage of the protection that comes when we involve others through personal accountability.

I was walking through a particularly difficult situation with a departing staff member. My temptations were clear: bitterness, anger, resentment, and the overwhelming desire to slander the person's name and reputation. A bit dark, I know, but it's true. While

I was frightened at the strength of sin's appeal, I still came up with all sorts of rationalizations. Oh, how I felt justified.

By God's grace I had enough sense to see the evil in my soul, and as a result I invited three other staff members to hold me accountable on my actions and dealings with this person. They were to monitor what I said in public, what I murmured in private, how I handled the practical matters of the departure itself, and how well I took the lead in conflict resolution in the spirit of biblical community.

The involvement of those three people proved decisive. Time and again they gave correction, encouragement, counsel, and prayer. The staff member's eventual departure turned from a nasty confrontation to an almost textbook example of staff transition. If left to myself though, I can only fear what might have happened.

I no longer struggled with the temptation to get revenge after this staff member left. But some temptations linger, staring us in the face over long periods of time. We need help in resisting these ongoing temptations. One well-known Christian leader regularly meets with a group of fellow pastors who challenge one another with the following seven questions:

1. Have you been with a woman anywhere this past week that might be seen as compromising?
2. Have any of your financial dealings lacked integrity?
3. Have you exposed yourself to any sexually explicit material?
4. Have you spent adequate time in Bible study and prayer?
5. Have you given priority time to your family?

6. Have you fulfilled the mandates of your calling?

7. Have you just lied to me?

CONFESSION AND REPENTANCE

For those times when we fail to resist temptation in its early stages, we can seize the *kairos* nature of the moment by investing fully in confession and repentance. The more we fall to our knees in confession, the more sensitized we become to sin in our lives and see it for what it is. As we grow in sensitivity, we grow increasingly aware of the subtle ploys of the Evil One amid the earliest rumblings of temptation's presence.

In addition to confession, we need to use prayer to request a critical intervention from God. When we ask Him to convict us of the sin in our lives, He opens our eyes to our sin. He also burdens us with its weight, and He prompts us to confess it and turn away from it.

The goal is sin sensitivity—to have a life and attitude that is acutely aware of sin in its many forms and its earliest stages. Not in a way that is neurotic, just in a way that brings a heightened awareness. Then we'll feel that early prick of the conscience and bring it before God in order to confess and repent. As Gordon MacDonald has reflected, "Many of us assume the first mark of growth in the Christian life to be better behavior.... [T]he first mark of maturity is actually the ability to identify and admit to bad behavior."[24]

That's why the Bible says, "Let us examine our ways and test them, and let us return to the LORD."[25]

As we live our lives, it's important to realize that every street has two sides. The oldest church in Amsterdam, the Oude Kerk, was built in 1366. Across the street from this venerable house of worship sits an outpost for the world's oldest profession. Seminude prostitutes display themselves from street-level windows around the church square and along the surrounding canals. For nearly six centuries, Amsterdam's infamous red-light district has surrounded its oldest institution of faith.

When I was in the Netherlands, I stood in the street, captivated by the stark symbolism of the scene. Church bells pealing on my left, the calls from women to come their way on my right. I glanced in the direction of the alluring voices, but my eyes didn't linger. I could see beyond the false illusion to the road that lay beyond, a road to a ruined life, accessed by a single moment of turning in its direction.

And then I *ran.*

9

WHEN NEEDING TO REPENT

"Jim, Scott left, and I don't know what to do."

It was Belinda. Her husband, Scott, was a deacon at the church I was pastoring while in seminary.

Instantly I asked, "What do you mean by 'left'? Is he missing?"

"No," she cried. "I mean he left *us*."

Scott had deserted his wife and their two young children. He simply gathered up a few belongings and moved into an apartment with another woman. Belinda asked if there was anything I could do.

I searched some class notes but didn't find anything that spelled out what to do in such situations. Still, I knew I had to get involved. I tried phoning Scott at the hospital where he worked. They took a message, but he never returned my call.

Finally I went to the hospital and asked for Scott to be paged. Not the most subtle approach, but I was young. Scott appeared in the hallway, and before he could head the other way I cornered him.

"I know why you're here," he said, "and it won't do any good."

"Scott, what in the world are you thinking?"

"I've left Belinda," he said. "And I'm not going back."

"But she's your wife. And you have children!"

"I know," he said, "but I don't care."

I was floored. "How could you not care? What about your responsibilities?"

"What about them? Right now I'm happy, and I don't want to give this up. I know it's wrong, but I don't care. If that means I'll burn in hell, then I guess I'll burn in hell."

He actually said that to me.

To this day I can feel the chill that ran down my spine as I stood in a hospital corridor with a man who'd given himself over to sin without regret and without remorse. He turned his back on what was right and deliberately embraced a terrible evil. I was no saint, and I'm still not. But to this day Scott's boldness in doing what he knew to be wrong astounds me.

Human Depravity

We're all on a first-name basis with sin. Not just minor, second-rate sin, but downright, hard-core moral rebellion. Everything from addictions to an uncontrolled tongue, a judgmental spirit to rampant materialism, cut-loose pride to a lack of generosity. Adultery is a biggie, to be sure. But it's just one sin among many. We all are sinners. Present tense. Today. Multiple times.

One of the most honest statements I've ever read was from French thinker Joseph de Maistre, who said, "I do not know what the heart of a rascal may be; I know what is in the heart of an honest man; it is horrible."[1] Or as Alexander Whyte said to a woman who praised him for his many good deeds: "Madam, if you knew the man I really was, you would spit in my face."[2] He wasn't confessing to hypocrisy; he was pointing out the reality of human depravity.

As Christians, we are redeemed by Christ and engaged in the ongoing process of being transformed. But we are sinners nonetheless. So it makes sense that what we do when we are confronted with our sin defines our life. In the aftermath of failure, when deciding what to do about our sin, we encounter a *kairos* moment.

There are many ways to react when we become aware of our sin. We can minimize it, try to justify it, overlook it, or deal with it. If it is left unaddressed, or is addressed inadequately, it will lead to more sin, coupled with an ever-increasing callousness to the severity of our actions. Without the intervention of repentance, the damaging consequences that flow from a life lived outside of God's design will mount.

Repentance is the solution to our natural tendency to sin. But here's the rub: The typical person of faith has no idea what it means to repent. We confuse all sorts of emotions and efforts with solid, life-giving, biblical repentance. So to clarify the true meaning of repentance, let's turn again to the life of David. It's fitting that the man we examined in the previous chapter for moral failure should have a chance to tell this side of the tale as well.

HOW TO REALIZE OUR OWN SIN

When we're in the midst of sin, it's often difficult to *see* the sin. Or perhaps more honestly, we've made the choice not to see it. But before we can repent, we must first realize that we have indeed sinned.

If we're blind to our misdeeds though, how can we realize that we're living in a state of sin? Faithful to our soul development, God always will bring the conviction of sin to bear. In David's case, it was rather dramatic:

> The LORD sent Nathan to David. When he came to him, he said, "There were two men in a certain town, one rich and the other poor. The rich man had a very large number of sheep and cattle, but the poor man had nothing except one little ewe lamb he had bought. He raised it, and it grew up with him and his children. It shared his food, drank from his cup and even slept in his arms. It was like a daughter to him.
>
> "Now a traveler came to the rich man, but the rich man refrained from taking one of his own sheep or cattle to prepare a meal for the traveler who had come to him. Instead, he took the ewe lamb that belonged to the poor man and prepared it for the one who had come to him."
>
> David burned with anger against the man and said to Nathan, "As surely as the LORD lives, the man who did this

deserves to die! He must pay for that lamb four times over, because he did such a thing and had no pity."

Then Nathan said to David, "You are the man! This is what the LORD, the God of Israel, says: 'I anointed you king over Israel, and I delivered you from the hand of Saul. I gave your master's house to you, and your master's wives into your arms. I gave you the house of Israel and Judah. And if all this had been too little, I would have given you even more. Why did you despise the word of the LORD by doing what is evil in his eyes? You struck down Uriah the Hittite with the sword and took his wife to be your own. You killed him with the sword of the Ammonites. Now, therefore, the sword will never depart from your house, because you despised me and took the wife of Uriah the Hittite to be your own.'"[3]

David either couldn't see his wrongdoing or chose not to see it. He'd hardened his heart and walled up his conscience. Saint John of the Cross noted that people tend to "measure God by themselves and not themselves by God, acting quite contrarily to that which He Himself taught."[4] To get through to the king, God had Nathan tell David a story about a little lamb. David had been a shepherd and still carried a shepherd's heart, so this was no mere tale. It struck the remaining nerves of his conscience and emotions, not to mention his lingering sense of justice and morality. David was repulsed and enraged by the rich man's evil. But then came the unexpected indictment: "You are the man!"

David had pursued Bathsheba then tried to cover up his adultery with lies and deceit—even the murder of her husband—and to this point hadn't even broken stride. How could a man after God's own heart lie in sin with another man's wife then have the other husband killed and not be stricken with guilt? Because sin can desensitize us. The more we turn away from doing what is right, the more callous and deadened we become. As C. S. Lewis's fictitious demon Screwtape observed of his human patient, "The more often he feels without acting, the less he will be able ever to act, and, in the long run, the less he will be able to feel."[5]

The great prophet Jeremiah conveyed the assessment of God toward such a spirit:

> This is what the LORD says:…"Why…have these people
> turned away?… They cling to deceit; they refuse to
> return.… No one repents of his wickedness, saying, 'What
> have I done?' Each pursues his own course.… Since they
> have rejected the word of the LORD, what kind of wisdom
> do they have?… 'Peace, peace,' they say, when there is no
> peace. Are they ashamed of their loathsome conduct? No,
> they have no shame at all; they do not even know how to
> blush."[6]

Confession and repentance work in the opposite way. The more we practice them, the more aware we become of the sin in our lives in all its forms. In contrast, David had become *de*sensitized. It took a direct confrontation with a prophet from God to awaken his conscience, just as it often takes a direct hit from the Holy Spirit in our lives for us to see our own sin. Other times it takes a crisis or a heart-wrenching loss or a shattering scandal. Like David, we should have known better, but the absence of repentance deadened us to the seriousness of our actions.

A Spiritual Vision Problem

The lack of repentance is only one reason David needed a visit from a prophet. Nathan told the king about another man's wrongdoing because we never see the horror or the shame of our own sin with as much clarity as when we see it in the lives of others. David's problem wasn't just the deadened spiritual nerve endings that resulted from his unrighteous choices. He also shared the carnal nature of being able to see the severity of sin in others but not in his own life. David wasn't just apathetic; he had a spiritual vision problem.

If you use reading glasses, you know the limitations of being farsighted. You can see things far away with clarity, but the words in a book or newspaper, anything up close, gets a bit fuzzy. Not everyone is farsighted physically, but no one is excluded from its spiritual counterpart. That's why the Bible and church history are full of examples demonstrating the need for outside spiritual support, accountability, and direction. Given our spiritual vision problem, it's the only way we'll be able to see the inward truth and reality about our own lives.

David knew that adultery, lying, and murder were wrong. But he couldn't see his actions falling into those categories. He took Bathsheba as his wife, didn't he? And yes, her husband was killed, but men die in battle every day. David may have arranged for Uriah's presence on the front line, but somebody had to lead the charge. David lacked all objectivity about the moral condition of his own life.

We're not all that different in the condition of our spiritual eyesight. That's why we need the intervention of others, as well as the conviction of the Holy Spirit. Søren Kierkegaard observed that "here in the temporal order, in the unrest, in the noise, in the pressure of the mob, in the crowd,…the voice of conscience becomes merely one voice among many." Yet, he continued, "in eternity, conscience is the only voice that is heard."[7]

The apostle Paul once wrote a letter to confront certain individuals in the city of Corinth about behavior patterns that were far from pleasing to God. The rebuke hurt, but it was necessary. He even touched on it again in a subsequent letter, with words that deliver a needed reminder to us today:

> I know I distressed you greatly with my letter. Although I
> felt awful at the time, I don't feel at all bad now that I see
> how it turned out. The letter upset you, but only for a
> while. Now I'm glad—not that you were upset, but that you
> were jarred into turning things around. You let the distress
> bring you to God, not drive you from him. The result was
> all gain, no loss.

Distress that drives us to God does that. It turns us around. It gets us back in the way of salvation. We never regret that kind of pain. But those who let distress drive them away from God are full of regrets, end up on a deathbed of regrets.[8]

HOW TO DEAL WITH SIN

When we finally become aware of our sin, we generally move through three stages, beginning with regret, continuing through remorse, and ending in repentance. The first emotion we experience following the realization of our sin is regret.

Regret

Genuine sorrow over our sin doesn't come immediately. First, we feel regret. We wish we hadn't done what we did, and we try to make up for it. David came to rue his adultery and his subsequent attempts at a cover-up, and he did all he could to make the best of the situation. Unfortunately, regret by itself rarely penetrates to our spirit. Rather than leading to repentance, it's more a reaction to getting caught or having to pay for what we did. It's an emotional reaction to the consequences we are facing, not so much a feeling of remorse over the act itself.

I was traveling in another country and heard about a well-known man who lost his position due to a long-term extramarital affair. When a friend of mine was asked to help mediate the situation, he wanted to know if the man came forward of his own accord to confess or if the affair had simply been discovered. In other words, the mediator was asking if this was mostly a *regret* thing—the man's adultery had been discovered, and now he wanted to land on his feet—or if it was something deeper that revealed the man's response to an inner sense of moral integrity.

Regret alone is not enough. Listen again to Kierkegaard: "This kind of repentance is selfish, a matter of the senses, sensually powerful for the moment, excited in expression,...[it] would drink down all the bitterness of sorrow in a single draught and then hurry on. It wants to get away from guilt."[9]

Remorse

It's necessary to move beyond regret into remorse, since that's when we experience spiritual sorrow. This is not anguish over the personal consequences of our actions as much as it is agony that we did a wrong thing in the eyes of God. This is the essence of spiritual remorse. It's having our heart break because we've broken God's heart.

I've worked with countless people who admit they've taken a "less than best" course of action. They're quick to express regret. What's missing is any sense of anguish that they've done something *wrong*. Instead there's an almost militant spirit that seeks to justify their course of action as both understandable and unavoidable.

Albert Camus, in his novel *The Fall*, observed that "each of us insists on being innocent at all cost, even if he has to accuse the whole human race and heaven itself."[10] Remorse over our sin is essential, but it isn't the highest or deepest place a soul can travel.

Repentance

The final destination of the soul when responding to sin is repentance. This is when we realize the wrong that we've done, we regret it, we experience authentic remorse over it, and then we proceed in a different direction. The word *repent* means "to turn around." To repent is to be heading in one direction, realize that it's the wrong way, and with regret and remorse turn around and head where we should have been going all along.

One of the easiest habits to fall into is the repetitive cycle of confession that seeks forgiveness over and over again without ever moving into repentance. We commit a sin, so we confess it and ask God to forgive us. Again and again. This can't be all we do to address the sin in our life. We must move on to repentance. To truly repent isn't simply the seeking of forgiveness; it's stopping, correcting, quitting, and fixing. In a word, repentance involves *changing.*

This is what David did. The Bible even records his prayer to God reflecting the dynamics of his repentance.

> Have mercy on me, O God,
>   according to your unfailing love;
>   according to your great compassion
>   blot out my transgressions.

Wash away all my iniquity
    and cleanse me from my sin.

For I know my transgressions,
    and my sin is always before me.[11]

Hear the realization of his own sin? Next comes the regret and remorse.

Against you, you only, have I sinned
    and done what is evil in your sight,
so that you are proved right when you speak
    and justified when you judge.
Surely I was sinful at birth,
    sinful from the time my mother conceived me.
Surely you desire truth in the inner parts;
    you teach me wisdom in the inmost place.[12]

No rationalizations, no cop-outs, no excuses. Just personal spiritual honesty. That was the truth in his "inmost parts" that he now understood. He knew what was hanging in the balance. He knew the *kairos* nature of what this page in time could read.

Cleanse me with hyssop, and I will be clean;
    wash me, and I will be whiter than snow.
Let me hear joy and gladness;

let the bones you have crushed rejoice.
Hide your face from my sins
    and blot out all my iniquity.[13]

Now comes the critical moment. Will he move all the way to repentance? The answer, reflected in this prayer, is a resounding yes.

Create in me a pure heart, O God,
    and renew a steadfast spirit within me.
Do not cast me from your presence
    or take your Holy Spirit from me.
Restore to me the joy of your salvation
    and grant me a willing spirit, to sustain me.

Then I will teach transgressors your ways,
    and sinners will turn back to you.
Save me from bloodguilt, O God,
    the God who saves me,
    and my tongue will sing of your righteousness.
O Lord, open my lips,
    and my mouth will declare your praise.
You do not delight in sacrifice, or I would bring it;
    you do not take pleasure in burnt offerings.
The sacrifices of God are a broken spirit;
    a broken and contrite heart,
    O God, you will not despise.[14]

Every line drips with David's resolve to lay his broken life on God's altar as a living sacrifice. The realization of his sin led to regret and quickly turned into remorse. Then came the butterfly emerging from the cocoon as repentance swept over his soul, for through repentance came a pure heart; an inner, steadfast spirit; a life in God's presence; the filling of the Holy Spirit; a life of joy; and a willing spirit. And flowing from that, a life that would have a positive impact on others.

WHAT FORGIVENESS MEANS

Once you seek forgiveness and repent, what then? You are forgiven, and you need to walk in that forgiveness. Accept and apply the grace you've been given. As Corrie ten Boom once said, when God forgives us, He takes our sins to the deepest part of the ocean, attaches a large weight, drops them overboard, and puts up a "No Fishing" sign.

But that's often easier said than done. The feelings of guilt and shame rarely just vaporize. They linger on like a bad odor, affecting every area of our lives, making us question how much God really accepts us.

I once read of a medical report that described how amputees experience the sensation of a phantom limb. They will have lost an arm or a leg, but somewhere, locked in their brains, a memory lingers of that limb, a memory so strong that they can feel their missing toes curl or their amputated hand grasp.[15] God doesn't want us to feel phantom guilt over sins that are no longer there. The Bible tells us, "This is how we shall know that we are children of the truth and can reassure ourselves in the sight of God, even if our own conscience makes us feel guilty. For God is greater than our conscience, and he knows everything."[16]

But what if we repeat the same sin? No matter how authentic the repentance, we may fall prey to the temptation again. And if that happens, we may wonder what this means for our relationship with God.

There are two extremes to avoid. The first is presumption. We should never minimize the severity of our sins and say, "Oops, sorry God. I guess I kind of blew it this time. Well, you know, boys will be boys!"

When we presume upon God's forgiveness, we forget that God is not mocked, and grace must never be cheapened. Paying for our sin cost Jesus His very life, and the call on our lives is plain: "You must be holy because I am holy."[17]

Equally distorted would be to forget the scandalously inexhaustible depth of grace that God is only too willing to bestow upon authentically repentant men and women. The wonder and joy of this can be found in Psalm 32. It's worth a read:

> Count yourself lucky, how happy you must be—
>> you get a fresh start,
>> your slate's wiped clean.
> Count yourself lucky—
>> GOD holds nothing against you

and you're holding nothing back from him.

When I kept it all inside,

>my bones turned to powder,

>my words became daylong groans.

The pressure never let up;

>all the juices of my life dried up.

Then I let it all out;

>>I said, "I'll make a clean breast of my failures to
GOD."

Suddenly the pressure was gone—

>my guilt dissolved,

>my sin disappeared.[18]

I read an old story about a man who'd been involved in a particular pattern of sin for years. As hard as he tried to stop, he kept
committing the sin. One day he went to God and said, "Lord, I
could just die with shame. Again and again I have done this thing.
I confess it to You and promise that I will never, *ever* sin this way
again. Will You forgive me?"

From heaven came the words, "I forgive you. It is all forgotten.
You are clean to start over again."

The man felt wonderfully free. God had forgiven him. What
more could he ask? All afternoon he rejoiced in the forgiveness, and
he committed himself to never fall into that same sin again.

Then, that night, temptation came his way, and he failed. He
could hardly bring himself to pray. Hadn't it been that very morning that he'd promised God he would never sin that way again?

He was so disgusted that he almost decided not to even try to deal with it. He'd just let his heart grow hard, or else he'd pretend that God somehow wouldn't notice his repeated sin. But he couldn't pretend, so once again he came to God in prayer and said, "God, I'm so embarrassed that I can hardly talk to You. I did it again."

"Did what?" God answered.

"You know. That sin," the man said. "The one we talked about this morning."

God replied, "I don't remember any sin."[19]

Our heavenly Father forgets our sin once He forgives it. But Satan will do what he can to muddy the waters. He's earned his reputation as the great accuser.

Here's what happens. The Holy Spirit convicts us of sin in our life. We handle it in a God-honoring way, moving through realization and regret, remorse and repentance. After that process has come to fruition, Satan will move in and accuse us of the sin we've already dealt with.

"Who do you think you are? You call yourself a Christian? No Christian would ever do what you did. You don't really think you and God are just going to be 'okay' after that, do you?"

We must learn to discern the difference between the voice of the Evil One and the voice of the Holy Spirit. When it comes to sin, the Holy Spirit will convict but never accuse. Satan has only one note to sing, and he uses it for the monotone chant of indictment. He'll do anything to keep us from experiencing that new lease on life that comes with repentance.

A PICTURE OF GRACE

Writer Philip Yancey tells of a young girl who grew up on a cherry orchard outside Traverse City, Michigan. Her parents tended to overreact to her nose rings, her harsh-sounding music, and her short skirts. They grounded her a few times, but that did little to change her attitude or her lifestyle. One night, when her father knocked on her door after an argument, she screamed "I hate you" and ran away.

She headed for Detroit, where she met a man who drove the biggest car she'd ever seen. He bought her lunch and provided her with a place to stay. He even gave her some pills that made her feel better than she'd ever felt before. She realized she'd been right all along: Her parents had been keeping her from all the fun.

Soon the man began to teach her what men like. Since she was underage, they paid a premium for her. She lived in a penthouse and ordered room service whenever she wanted.

After about a year, the first signs of illness began to appear. Suddenly her boss turned mean. He couldn't risk having anyone around who was that sick, so he threw her out on the street. She was able to turn a couple of tricks a night, but they didn't pay much. And all the money went to support her drug habit.

When winter came, she found herself sleeping on metal grates outside the big department stores. "Sleeping" was the wrong word though. A teenage girl alone at night in downtown Detroit can never relax. One night, as she lay in fear of the sound of approaching footsteps, everything about her life suddenly looked different.

She felt like a little girl, lost in a cold and frightening city. She began to cry. She was hungry, and she needed a fix.

Then a wonderful picture filled her mind. It was May in her hometown with a million cherry trees in bloom, and her golden retriever was chasing a tennis ball.

"God, why did I leave? My dog back home eats better than I do."

She started to cry, knowing that more than anything else in the world, she wanted to go home. She walked to a phone booth and dialed the number. Three straight calls, three connections to the answering machine. The third time she left a message.

"Dad, Mom, it's me. I was wondering about maybe coming home. I'm catching a bus up your way, and it'll get there about midnight tomorrow. If you're not at the station, well, I guess I'll just stay on the bus until it hits Canada."

It took seven hours for the bus to make all the stops between Detroit and the girl's hometown, and during that time all she could think about were the flaws in her plan. What if her parents were out of town and didn't get the message? What if they were home but she hadn't given them enough time to arrange to meet her at the bus station? What if they didn't want her back?

Then she began to rehearse what to say, things like, "Dad, I'm sorry. I know I was wrong. It's not your fault; it's all mine. Dad, can you forgive me?" She said the words over and over.

When the bus finally rolled into the station, the driver announced, "Traverse City, Michigan. Fifteen-minute stop." Fifteen minutes for her entire life to be decided.

She walked into the terminal not knowing what to expect. But none of the images that raced through her mind matched the scene that awaited her. Just inside the bus station stood a group of forty relatives: brothers and sisters, great-aunts and uncles and cousins, a grandmother and even a great-grandmother. They all were wearing goofy party hats and blowing noisemakers. And taped to one wall of the terminal was a banner that said, "Welcome home!"

Then out of the crowd stepped her dad. Through tears, she started to say, "Dad, I'm sorry. I know…"

But he interrupted her. "Hush, child. We've got no time for that. You'll be late for the party. A banquet's waiting for you at home."[20]

This young girl's story is a retelling of Jesus' parable about the prodigal son. She turned away from God, found out her self-directed life wasn't really what she wanted, and chose *repentance*—a repentance that was met not with rejection or condemnation, but with forgiveness and grace.

And it changed her entire life. It was, after all, a *kairos* moment.

10

WHEN DECIDING ON GOD

A four-year-old girl, soon after her brother was born, asked her parents to leave her alone for a little while with the baby. They worried that she was jealous of the little boy and might want to pinch him or shake him. So they told her that she needed to be with Mommy and Daddy when she was alone with the baby. They started watching her for signs of jealousy, but such signs never appeared. Instead, every indicator pointed to a sincere love for her baby brother.

Still, the little girl asked to be left *alone* with the infant, so finally the parents allowed it. They let her go into the nursery by herself, leaving the door open enough to keep an eye on her. The girl walked up to her baby brother, put her face close to his, and quietly said, "Baby, tell me what God feels like, because I'm starting to forget."[1]

Do you remember what God feels like? Have you *ever* known?

When it comes to life-defining moments, this one matters more than all the rest.

Life Without God

The latter part of the twentieth century was marked by denial, and it was painful to watch. We denied our limits. Women entered the work force in mass numbers, and we talked of the superwoman who could bring home the bacon and then fry it up in the pan. Women tried to be the perfect mom, the perfect wife, the perfect employee. They wanted to have the perfect house, prepare the perfect meals, and maintain the perfect figure.

They ended up with the perfect prescription: Prozac.

Men, of course, were headed in the same direction. We believed we could climb the corporate ladder quicker than our colleagues, cover all the bases at home, and still get in eighteen holes of golf every Saturday. Both sexes kept burning the candle at both ends because we were in denial of the truth that we simply couldn't do everything. We didn't even want to think that we might be getting older, and we certainly wouldn't concede that getting older would have any noticeable effect on us. The first wave of baby boomers started entering their fifties during the 1990s, and it wasn't pretty. We were all a bit like Arnold Schwarzenegger who, at fifty-four, immediately after he went through an aortic valve replacement, decided he could get on a LifeCycle and work out. He blew out his new heart valve, forcing the surgeons to perform his operation a second time.[2]

We were also in denial about guilt. Anne Lamott writes about a doctor friend who used to shoot up sodium pentothal in his garage and then make a run for the bedroom, where he could pass out for the night. He was convinced he had a problem with insomnia, not drugs. Another friend, an admitted alcoholic, had to have surgery to remove pebbles from his forehead. The tiny stones got embedded when he smashed his face into the pavement at the end of a cocaine binge. When he told Lamott about his operation, he was angry because now people were going to think he had a drug problem.[3]

But as ridiculous as all this sounds, none of it compares to our denial about God.

During the nineties, people began asking spiritual questions. They started a spiritual search and pursued a deep desire to develop themselves spiritually. But then it got messy. They found that America had opened a supernatural supermarket. Religious groups, sects, cults, movements, philosophies, and world-views abounded in incredible numbers and staggering diversity. When it came to an authoritative spiritual text, there was the Bible, the Bhagavad-Gita, the Koran, and the Book of Mormon. When it came to religious leaders, you could select from the pope, the Dalai Lama, Buddha, or Muhammad. When it came to religious groups, you could align with Jehovah's Witnesses, the New Age movement, Islam, Judaism, Christianity, or Scientology.

Then, just for fun, we decided to add a new value to our cultural milieu: the conviction that all roads lead to the same God. We decided that the old assertion that only one way was right and all the other ways were wrong was narrow-minded and bigoted. We became convinced that searching for God was a lot like climbing a mountain. Everyone knows there is not just *one* way to climb a mountain—mountains are much too big for that. When scaling a peak, any number of paths can be taken that will get you to the top. Likewise, the various ideas about God are like different ways up a mountain. Or as a rabbi and a priest teamed up to conclude, all the names of God in all the world's religions name the same God.[4]

This thinking led many seekers to stop looking for ultimate spiritual truth as well as for the one, true God. Instead the search has become a self-made affair, with spiritual beliefs being hand-picked according to personal preference. We walk along the celestial food bar, see all that's there, and put on our plate whatever looks good today. A real God, with a set identity, need not be considered. Or even worse, we conclude that He isn't even around.

The end of the twentieth century was marked by an ironic embrace of a transcendent and mystical spirituality that was devoid of God. A resurgent practice of ancient paganism, offering supernatural experiences without a supreme being, was popularized through crystals, spirit beings, witchcraft, and vampires. We were offered vaguely defined powers and forces, the spiritual and the metaphysical, rituals and rites, but with one amazing omission. God was left out of the mix.

When you deny your limits or deny your guilt, you can wreck your life. But when you deny God, you can lose your very soul. Even if you call yourself a Christian.

During the nineties, historian Mark Noll released a book that sounded something of a wake-up call to evangelical Christians. Noll declared, "The scandal of the evangelical mind is that there is not much of an evangelical mind."[5] Yet there is an even greater scandal afoot, the scandal of evangelical *belief*. As a result of the denial that permeates our day, even those who believe they embrace the Christian faith may, in fact, not grasp it at all.

TOUGH QUESTIONS

There is no greater *kairos* moment than when you decide on having God *be* God. Nothing carries more weight or presents deeper implications for defining your life. Because of this, we must strip away all pretense and posturing. Anything that presents itself as a true decision for God that, in fact, *isn't* must be ruthlessly exposed. Without doing that, we'll never be able to enter into a true relationship with God.

To help you lay hold of this pivotal moment, consider these four questions.

1. You say you believe, but is it by the Book or by your own set of rules?

One summer while studying at Oxford University, I was invited to a reception for visiting students. Within the first five minutes, I found myself in conversation with two women, one from Florida, the other from California. After exchanging the usual pleasantries, I was asked what I did for a living. I told them I was a pastor studying in England for the summer.

The woman from Florida seemed primed for the moment.

"Well, I'm glad somebody like you is at a place like this so that you can give people the truth. You know, the *real* story. Why don't more ministers do that?"

"Well," I said, "I'm not sure I know what you're talking about."

"You know, all of that stuff about Jesus having died on a cross, resurrected on the third day, and all the miracles. I mean, He never died. In fact, He lived a long, full life, got married, and had kids."

"Oh, really?" I said.

"Don't you believe that?" She was incredulous.

I had just met this woman, and I didn't want to immediately get into it with her, but this was a bit much. "I'm sure there are those who might agree with you, but I have to tell you that I'm not one of them."

"You mean you believe all of that stuff in the Bible?"

"Yes," I replied.

"You mean, like the Virgin Birth?"

"Yes," I said.

You could see it written all over her face. Here's this seemingly intelligent guy studying at Oxford, but he says he believes the Bible. What's wrong with this picture?

Our conversation went on in earnest but with a fascinating twist. While the woman from Florida continued to ask questions and raise objections, her friend from California joined with me to try to explain that perhaps some of the sources for her reconstruction of Jesus and the Christian faith were less than sound.

"So," I said to my new ally, "would you consider yourself a Christian?"

"No," she said.

Then to my surprise, the woman with whom I'd been debating said, "Well, *I* would."

Our confused spiritual values have brought us to this point. The woman who tended to agree with my view didn't call herself a Christian, but the woman who opposed a biblical view of Christ did.

The Christian faith is not simply a defined world-view, but a personal, life-changing faith that is based on divine revelation. It's not simply a religious organization governed by a set of rules. It's a community of faith comprised of people who believe that God has revealed Himself and the truth about Himself through Scripture and, dramatically and completely, in Christ. The life of Christ shows us things about God that could not otherwise be known.

Through divine revelation, which literally means the "drawing back of the curtain," we are shown the spiritual reality behind the physical reality that we experience through our five senses. As a result, the foundation of any relationship with God can only be based on revealed truth about God, as opposed to our own theological stylings. The challenge this brings can be disconcerting for those who consider themselves under the mantle of Christianity yet find themselves at odds with what the Christian faith maintains.

A seminary professor of mine once served on the Faith and Order Commission of the National Council of Churches, which prepared a paper outlining how the Unification Church, better known as the Moonies, differed from Christianity. After the paper was published, my professor received a phone call from an irate woman who was part of the Unification Church.

"You can't say that someone isn't a Christian, and you can't say that our organization isn't Christian!" she insisted.

To which my professor replied, "Madam, if you cannot say that anything is *not* Christian, then you have no grounds for saying that anything *is* Christian."

The Christian faith is not open for amendment. At its heart is a God who is not only there, but who has not been silent. The Bible is not simply another book, inspired along the same lines as an exciting John Grisham novel. The Bible claims to be the very Word of God. In like manner, Jesus was not just another good man, a great teacher or mere prophet, along the lines of Gandhi or Buddha. He claimed to be God in human form. He must be accepted or rejected on those grounds. You can't construct your own version of Jesus and consider yourself an authentic Christian.

2. You say you believe, but are you playing the game or simply watching from the stands?

When I was in college, I attended a series of lectures that dealt with building a strong and lasting marriage. Every Sunday evening for six weeks, I immersed myself in the world of matrimony. I learned principles and procedures, skills and Scriptures that directed the life of a husband.

One small problem. I wasn't married.

It was great to know how to communicate with my wife, work through marital conflict, and nurture intimacy. But to have any of that knowledge come to life would have to involve standing at the altar with someone and saying "I do."

Christianity is not a spectator sport. You're either in the game or not a part of what's happening. You can't just sit and look on from the grandstands.

When the apostle Paul attempted to describe the dynamics of the Christian faith, his search for analogies returned him time and again to that of an athletic contest:

> Do you not know that in a race all the runners run, but only one gets the prize? Run in such a way as to get the prize. Everyone who competes in the games goes into strict training.... Therefore I do not run like a man running aimlessly; I do not fight like a man beating the air. No, I beat my body and make it my slave so that after I have preached to others, I myself will not be disqualified for the prize.[6]

Here we must remind ourselves of James's uncomfortable declaration that faith without works is dead. "What good is it, my brothers, if a man claims to have faith but has no deeds? Can such faith save him?"[7] James supplies the answer: "faith by itself, if it is not accompanied by action, is dead."[8] The claim to faith, if devoid of action, draws the proclaimed faith into question. Action is to faith what breath is to life. Separated, there is little more than a cold corpse. A true relationship with Christ can't help but bring about significant change in your life. If there is no impact, then the presence of a true relationship is drawn into doubt. This is not about earning your salvation, but about a faith that bears the markings of authenticity. As the sixteenth-century reformer Martin Luther reminded us, we are saved by faith alone, but not by a faith that *is* alone.

3. You say you believe, but is Christ the steering wheel in your life or the spare tire?

Some of us have a relationship with God that results in little more than having Him tucked away in the trunk. We pull Him out when our life is brought to a standstill by a flat. The rest of the time, when things are running smoothly, He's locked away where He can't be seen or heard. Unless we're in the throes of a life crisis, we don't give Him much thought.

Yet Jesus said, "Anyone who intends to come with me has to let me lead. You're not in the driver's seat; *I* am."[9] Belief that is authentic speaks to every sphere of life, including our marriage, friendships, finances, vocation, and parenting. A true relationship with Christ is not an attachment, much less a category. It's an all-encompassing "followership" that reflects authentic faith. One only has to consider the haunting words of Jesus, which at the time of the Judgment will fall upon the ears of those who refused to follow His will: "I never knew you."[10]

4. You say you believe, but do you know Him or just know of Him?

Perhaps the most probing of all questions is the one that investigates the difference between *knowing* God and simply knowing *about* God. It's a critical question to consider, because it speaks to the difference between authentic faith and mere head knowledge. With more than a bit of biting sarcasm, James asks: "Do I hear you professing to believe in the one and only God, but then observe you complacently sitting back as if you had done something wonderful? That's just great. Demons do that, but what good does it do them? Use your heads!"[11]

Being a Christian is more than just intellectual assent. It's not what you know, but *Who* you know. It's not simply what's in your head, but what's in your heart. It's not about religion; it's about relationship. The late author and Christian counselor Brent Curtis suggested we think of the stark difference between cold knowledge and true intimacy by imagining taking a seat in a sidewalk café and overhearing a man and his fiancée talking.

"I'm so looking forward to our wedding day. I do love you so much," she begins. "I really wish I could see more of you. There's so much about you I want to know better."

"Yes, dear, I know," he monotones. "I'm going to send you a book that describes more about my life. I'm sure you'll get a lot out of it."

"Well, I'll be glad to read it," she says. "But I just want to hold your hand." Then, looking around mischievously, she says, "I just want to kiss you."

"I'm sure you do, beloved," comes the man's reply. "Let me send you a tape describing the role of physical affection at different stages of courtship. You'll find it worthwhile, I'm sure."

She looks at him in disbelief. Regrouping, she says, "That's wonderful, darling. It's just that I so look forward to our wedding day. I want to be with you so badly. I think of us being, you know, 'together,' day and night."

Her fiancé says, "Yes, I know. Intimacy is important. I'd like to send you to a weekend seminar that really should be quite helpful."[12]

About this time most of us would walk over to where these two lovebirds are sitting and tell the guy to get a heartbeat. He doesn't have a *clue* how to love this woman, much less how to be in a personal, ongoing relationship with her. But how many of us carry on our love relationship with God this way? The heart of the question is simple: Do we really love Him?

One of my favorite musicals is *Fiddler on the Roof,* the story of a Jewish peasant named Tevya who, along with his wife and daughters, lives in Russia just before the time of the Communist Revolution. There are so many emotions in play throughout the tale, such as the timeless tensions between the modern world and tradition, and the Jewish people and their oppressors. But it is first and foremost a love story. Love between Tevya's daughters and their young suitors, and as the story unfolds, love between Tevya and his wife.

After one of his daughters announces that she wants to go against tradition and marry the man she loves, bypassing the matchmaker's choice and her father's permission, Tevya is forced to look at his *own* marriage. He returns home to his wife and plaintively asks, "Golda, do you love me?"

"Do I what?" comes her reply.

"Do you love me?"

"Do I love you?"

"Well?"

Brushing aside his question, she sings: "With our daughters getting married, and there's trouble in the town, you're upset, you're worn out, go inside, go lie down. Maybe it's indigestion."

"Ah, no, Golda. I'm asking you a question! Do you love me?"

"You're a fool," is her only reply.

"I know," he says laughingly, but then returns again with earnestness, "but do you love me?"

"Do I love you?"

"Well?"

Regaining her composure, she responds, "For twenty-five years I've washed your clothes, cooked your meals, cleaned your house, given you children, milked your cow. After twenty-five years, why talk about love right now?"

"Golda," Tevya pleads, "the first time I met you was on our wedding day. I was scared."

"I was shy," she remembers.

"I was nervous," adds her husband.

"So was I," she agrees.

"But my father and my mother said we'd learn to love each other. And now I'm asking, Golda, do you love me?"

"I'm your wife!" she protests.

"I know! But do you love me?"

Then, almost to herself, she says, "Do I love him?"

"Well?"

"For twenty-five years I've lived with him, fought with him, starved with him. Twenty-five years my bed is his. If that's not love, what is?"

"Then you love me?"

Almost surprised at her answer, she says, "I suppose I do."

"And I suppose I love you, too," Tevya replies.

Then, tenderly by each other's side, they sing the final line together: "It doesn't change a thing, but even so...after twenty-five years, it's nice to know."[13]

But it did change things. And that's why God's ultimate question to you is the same: "Do you love Me?"

BEYOND LIFELESS BELIEF

With everything on the line, it's critical to know exactly how to seize the *kairos* moment of deciding upon God in such a way that you enter into a vital relationship with Him. Many of us believe in God, but that isn't enough. We need to experience God as leader, forgiver, and friend. The Bible shows us the way. For the sake of simplicity, let's examine a single verse that gives us the spiritual equation for what it means to become a Christian: "Yet to all who received him, to those who believed in his name, he gave the right to become children of God."[14] Take note of the three verbs in that verse and you have the equation: Believe + Receive = Become.[15] Let's look at these crucial actions one by one.

Believe. First, while belief itself is not enough, there does need to be an intellectual acceptance of the truth of Christianity. To believe is to embrace the propositional truths the Bible teaches about the saving work and message of Christ. Those truths are that Jesus was God Himself in human form. He came to earth to sacrifice Himself to pay for the wrongs we've committed. On the third day, He rose from the dead. And one day He will return to earth.

Receive. To the act of believing we must add the necessary step of receiving. You must accept God's free offer of forgiveness and eternal life. As with any gift, we must take what has been given, for until we do, it's not really ours. It can be offered, but we must reach out our hands to accept this free gift. There comes a time when you admit your sins, turn away from them and toward God, and gratefully accept Christ's payment for those sins on your behalf. There must be that conscious decision, that purposeful choice. This is a relationship you must knowingly, deliberately enter into.

And doing that is just one prayer away. For an idea of what that prayer might be like, consider this one:

Dear Lord Jesus:
I know that I am a sinner and need Your forgiveness. I
believe that You died for my sins. I want to turn from the

way I've been living. I now invite You to come into my heart and life. I want to trust You as my forgiver and follow You as my leader. Amen.

Become. Now the third part of the equation comes into play: You *become.* This is the life change that God works in you after you believe in Him and receive Him as your forgiver, leader, and friend. "What this means is that those who become Christians become new persons," wrote the apostle Paul. "They are not the same anymore, for the old life is gone. A new life has begun!"[16]

Much of that new life already has been navigated in the journey described in this book. Newness of life flows from seizing the ten *kairos* moments in obedience to God's direction and leadership. But to fulfill the journey and enjoy an eternal relationship of love and obedience, you need *God.*

A FINAL WORD

C. S. Lewis once observed that our earthly life is nothing more than shadows, masking the deep reality that will become blazingly alive and clear to us when we stand before the living God and face eternity. Yet it often can seem as if *this* life is everything, and that our spiritual decisions and commitments are the real shadows. Such a view leads us to enlarge the significance of this world and to diminish the importance of the decisions we make while in it.

There are two ways to look at life—one is horizontally and the other is vertically. To have horizontal vision means to look at what's around you, the here and now. You rarely, if ever, lift your gaze to the horizon beyond your experience. But looking at life with a vertical perspective is quite different. You not only see what's around you, but your sight also is infused with a sense that this life is not all there is. You see with crystal clarity that you have a soul, that you'll face an eternal existence. There is a deep realization that there's a God on the loose, and this life has more significance and a deeper meaning than simply to live and to die.

Imagine a tight, taught line that stretches across the room. Now take that line and picture it extending through the walls and outside the building. Carry the line out as far as you can see, in both directions, until it disappears over the horizon. If you could board a plane and take flight following the line in either direction, it would continue to stretch out in front of you. It would extend as far as you could see, not just wrapping itself around this world but reaching beyond our atmosphere, extending out through space, beyond our solar system, beyond our universe. The line is never-ending. Got the picture?

Now take a pen and on this line make a scratch. Just a small scratch. That lone scratch is your earthly life in the scope of eternity.

Now anyone with any sense would live his life in light of the eternal line. But too many of us don't. We make that little scratch *everything*. We lead scratch lives with scratch attitudes and scratch goals and scratch priorities.[1]

But that's not the pattern we see in the life of Jesus. The Bible tells us that He was infused with an eternal, vertical perspective on life. "Jesus knew that the Father had put all things under his power," observed Jesus' best friend while on earth, "and that he had come from God and was returning to God."[2]

You, too, are going to go to God. Your future does not consist of the remaining hours contained within the momentary blink of the tiny scratch on the eternal line. Your future *is* that line that extends ever onward. Viewed from that perspective, your earthly life makes up a single *kairos* moment, a moment that determines everything that will occur during the eternity that lies in wait. That's why Jesus, when asked by Peter if leaving everything to follow Him was going to be worth it, could give the following answer:

> I tell you the truth, at the renewal of all things, when the Son of Man sits on his glorious throne, you who have followed me,…everyone who has left houses or brothers or sisters or father or mother or children or fields for my sake will receive a hundred times as much and will inherit eternal life.[3]

Jesus promises that if we will follow Him, if we will make the investment of a life commitment, we will receive everything that ever has or ever will matter. *Everything.* Whatever you think following Jesus will cost you in this world, you will receive one hundred times as much in its place in the world to come. And not only that, but you'll enjoy eternal life in heaven.

GROUNDHOG DAY

In the movie *Groundhog Day,* Bill Murray plays a character forced to live February 2—Groundhog Day—over and over again. Every morning the alarm goes off at the same time, "I've Got You, Babe" blares over the radio, and the snowstorm that blows in that day keeps him from escaping the small town in which he's trapped.

Initially Murray concludes that life is a meaningless investment that results in little consequence, so he pursues a course of moral abandon. No matter what he says, what he does, or how he lives, the next day will be the same as the day before, untouched by the previous day's actions. So eat, drink, and be merry.

In the end he comes to a deep awareness that when time and our choices within time become meaningless, so does life. He determines to seize his one, solitary day, experimenting with different choices until he finds he has shaped the life-defining moments of that day to create the life he longs for. He finds that making the right choices, at the right times, even within a twenty-four-hour span, can alter the course of his life and the lives of everyone around him.

You have been given a series of *kairos* moments through which you can seize your day and create the life you long for. Going deeper, your life composes a single *kairos* moment in relation to God that will shape your eternal destiny, forever fulfilling the very longings of your heart.

Today is your Groundhog Day. Wake up and live its eternal potential.

NOTES AND ACKNOWLEDGMENTS

An Opening Word

1. Adapted from Kay McSpadden, "Choices Made Now, Foolish or Wise, Will Shape the Remains of Their Days," *Charlotte Observer*, 25 May 2000, sec. A, p. 13. McSpadden's students were discussing Kazuo Ishiguro's *The Remains of the Day* (London: Faber and Faber, 1989). Article excerpted by permission of the author.

2. Dewey Gram, based on a screenplay by David Franzoni, John Logan, and William Nicholson, *Gladiator* (New York: Onyx, 2000), 24.

3. The Greek language actually has a number of terms that express the experience of time, with the most extensive being *aion*, which refers to an extended period of time. *Chronos* refers to the quantitative, linear understanding of time. It is this formal, scientific understanding of time that is the most compatible with our modern use of the word. *Kairos*, however, refers to the *content* of time. For more on the background of this word, see Walter Bauer, *A Greek-English Lexicon of the New Testament and Other Early Christian Literature*, trans. William F. Arndt and F. Wilbur Gingrich (Chicago: University of Chicago Press, 1957), 394-5; Gerhard Kittel, ed., *Theological Dictionary of the New Testament*, trans. Geoffrey W. Bromiley, 10 vols. (Grand Rapids, Mich.: Eerdmans, 1964-76), 3:455-62; Colin Brown, ed., *The New International Dictionary of New Testament Theology*, 3 vols. (Grand Rapids, Mich.: Zondervan, 1975-78), 3:833-9.

4. Plato, *Republic 2*, trans. B. Jowett (New York: Walter J. Black, 1942), 269.

5. See Jeremiah 46:17.

6. See Luke 4:13.

7. See Luke 8:13.

8. See Luke 19:44. Of course, the great *kairos* moment within the biblical materials was the Incarnation itself, the moment of God's coming and the fulfillment of the redemptive drama.

9. As quoted by Michael J. Gelb, *How to Think Like Leonardo da Vinci* (New York: Delacorte Press, 1998), 97.

10. Os Guinness, *The American Hour* (New York: The Free Press, 1993), 396.

11. Excerpts from the script based on Touchstone Pictures' copyrighted feature film *Dead Poets Society* are used by permission from Disney Enterprises, Inc. The poem "To the Virgins to Make Much of Time" was written by Robert Herrick (1591–1674) and can be found unabridged in Laurence Perrine, *Literature: Structure, Sound, and Sense,* 3d ed. (New York: Harcourt Brace Jovanovich, 1978).

12. Ephesians 5:15-16; cf. Colossians 4:5

13. See Dorothy Bass, *Receiving the Day: Christian Practices for Opening the Gift of Time* (San Francisco: Jossey-Bass, 2000), 10.

Chapter 1

1. Numbers 20:8

2. Numbers 20:12

3. Robert Frost, "The Road Not Taken," in *The Poetry of Robert Frost,* ed. Edward Connery Lathem (New York: Holt, Rinehart and Winston, 1969), 105.

4. See Deuteronomy 34:1-4.

5. Romans 7:19

6. Adapted from "Vintage Voices," *Richardson Today* (city of Richardson, Texas, newsletter), November 1978, Vintage Voices section. Used by permission of the publisher.

7. See Acts 19:1-7.

8. Adapted from Edward K. Rowell, ed., *Fresh Illustrations from Leadership Journal* (Grand Rapids, Mich.: Baker, 1997), 100, which itself was adapted from an article on Penick in *Reader's Digest.*

9. John 14:23-24

10. Adapted from Donald McCullough, "Reasons to Fear Easter," Preaching Today, tape no. 116, acquired through Preaching Today.com/Christianity Today International.

11. 1 John 2:4-6

12. Dietrich Bonhoeffer, *The Cost of Discipleship*, rev. ed. (New York: Collier Books/MacMillan, 1963), 69.

13. Matthew 7:21-23, TLB

14. Jeremiah 6:15

15. Psalm 19:7-8,11, TLB

16. Psalm 119:105

17. James 1:5

18. See Proverbs 12:15.

19. Romans 10:11, NCV

20. C. S. Lewis, *The Screwtape Letters* (New York: Bantam, 1982), 36.

Chapter 2

1. Adapted from Henry Cloud and John Townsend, *Safe People* (Grand Rapids, Mich.: Zondervan, 1995), 62.

2. This list of questions was compiled from various sources. As such, many of them—if not all—are far from original with me.

3. Anne Lamott, *Traveling Mercies: Some Thoughts on Faith* (New York: Pantheon, 1999), 100.

4. As noted by Gerald G. May, *Addiction and Grace: Love and Spirituality in the Healing of Addictions* (San Francisco: Harper, 1988), 13.

5. Brent Curtis and John Eldredge, *The Sacred Romance: Drawing Closer to the Heart of God* (Nashville, Tenn.: Nelson, 1997), 73.

6. Genesis 2:18, NLT

7. Adapted from Les and Leslie Parrott, *Relationships* (Grand Rapids, Mich.: Zondervan, 1998), 14. See also Henry Cloud, *Changes That Heal* (New York: HarperPaperbacks, 1992), 55.

8. See Paul Stanley, *Connecting* (Colorado Springs, Colo.: NavPress, 1992).

9. Dietrich Bonhoeffer, *Life Together,* trans. John W. Doberstein (New York: Harper, 1954), 112.

10. Martin E. Marty, *Friendship* (Allen, Tex.: Argus, 1980), 7ff.

11. Larry Crabb, *Connecting: Healing for Ourselves and Our Relationships* (Nashville, Tenn.: Word, 1997), 99. For more on Crabb's excellent reflections on this issue, see *The Safest Place on Earth* (Nashville, Tenn.: Word, 1999).

12. Romans 15:7, Phillips

13. 1 Thessalonians 2:8

14. John 13:34

15. Richard Selzer, M.D., *Mortal Lessons: Notes in the Art of Surgery* (New York: Simon & Schuster, 1976), 45-6.

16. Colossians 3:13

17. 1 Thessalonians 5:11

18. Hebrews 10:24-25

19. I cannot locate the original version of this story, which I adapted. But I believe the physician in question was Sir William Osler.

20. James 5:16

21. Titus 1:13

22. John Powell, *Why Am I Afraid to Tell You Who I Am?* (Allen, Tex.: Thomas More, 1969), 11.

23. Ecclesiastes 4:9-10

24. Psalm 118:8

25. John 2:23-25, MSG

26. Cloud and Townsend, *Safe People,* 28-39.

27. Powell, *Why Am I Afraid to Tell You Who I Am?* 39.

28. Referenced in Douglas V. Steere, *On Being Present Where You Are* (Wellington, Pa.: Pendle Hill Pamphlet # 151, 1967), 14.

29. Steere, *On Being Present Where You Are,* 35.

30. "If I Had Only Known," words and music by Jana Stanfield and Craig Morris, copyright © 1991 Sony/ATV Tunes LLC and Jana StanTunes /Alabama Band Music (a division of Wildcountry, Inc.) (ASCAP). All rights on behalf of Sony/ATV Tunes LLC administered by Sony/ATV Music Publishing, 8 Music Square West, Nashville, TN 37203. All rights reserved. Used by permission.

Chapter 3

1. As cited by John Maxwell, *Failing Forward: Turning Mistakes into Stepping Stones for Success* (Nashville, Tenn.: Nelson, 2000), 4-5.

2. Proverbs 23:7, NASB

3. See 2 Corinthians 11:21-33.

4. Philippians 3:13-14

5. See James Belasco, *Teaching the Elephant to Dance* (New York: Crown, 1990).

6. Philippians 3:13, Phillips

7. John 3:17

8. Philippians 3:13, NLT

9. Philippians 1:6, NLT

10. Adapted from Warren Bennis and Burt Nanus, *Leaders* (New York: Harper & Row, 1985), 76.

11. See Neil Baldwin, *Edison: Inventing the Century* (New York: Hyperion, 1995).

12. See Maynard Solomon, *Mozart: A Life* (New York: HarperCollins, 1995).

13. See Simon Schama, *Rembrandt's Eyes* (New York: Knopf, 1999).

14. See Lee Cullum, *Genius Came Early: Creativity in the Twentieth Century* (Austin, Tex.: Windsor House Publishing, 1999), and Howard Gardner, *Creating Minds* (New York: Basic Books, 1993).

15. Philippians 3:14

16. Adapted from Charles Swindoll, *Growing Strong in the Seasons of Life* (Portland, Oreg.: Multnomah, 1983), 69-70. On Lincoln, see David Herbert Donald, *Lincoln* (New York: Simon & Schuster, 1995), and Stephen B. Oates, *With Malice Toward None: A Life of Abraham Lincoln* (New York: HarperPerennial, 1994).

17. 2 Corinthians 4:8-9, NLT

18. Hebrews 12:1-3, NLT

19. Adapted from John Maxwell, *Developing the Leader Within You* (Nashville, Tenn.: Nelson, 1993), 95.

20. Hebrews 12:1, NCV

21. As cited by Maxwell, *Failing Forward*, 53.

22. Hebrews 12:1, NLT

23. Adapted from the film *Rudy,* directed by David Anspaugh, released in 1993 by Columbia TriStar; as well as Maxwell, *Failing Forward*, 31-3. See also Rudy Ruettiger and Mike Celizic, *Rudy's Rules* (Waco, Tex.: WRS Publishing, 1995).

24. Adapted from Steven J. Lawson, *Men Who Win* (Colorado Springs, Colo.: NavPress, 1992), 156.

Chapter 4

1. Acts 13:36

2. Adapted from an address given by Charles Colson, "The Power of Christ's Gospel in Cultures Worldwide," delivered in August 2000 at Amsterdam 2000, Amsterdam, The Netherlands.

3. John 8:23-24, MSG

4. Esther 4:14

5. Proverbs 29:18, KJV

6. See James Emery White, *You Can Experience a Purposeful Life* (Nashville, Tenn.: Word, 2000).

7. Larry Crabb, *The Safest Place on Earth* (Nashville, Tenn.: Word, 1999), 63.

8. 1 John 3:1, Phillips

9. Philip Yancey, *The Bible Jesus Read* (Grand Rapids, Mich.: Zondervan, 1999), 177-8.

10. 2 Corinthians 6:18

11. Hebrews 12:7-10, MSG

12. Frederick Buechner, *Wishful Thinking* (New York: Harper & Row, 1973), 13.

13. Sharon Begley et al., "Decoding the Human Body," *Newsweek*, April 10, 2000, 50-7.

14. Ephesians 4:7, TLB

15. Romans 12:6, NLT

16. Psalm 139:13

17. Prompted by a news report on the club in the *Charlotte Observer*, 6 September 1993, sec. A, p. 4.

18. Psalm 37:4-5

19. Rick Warren, *The Purpose Driven Church* (Grand Rapids, Mich.: Zondervan, 1995), 370.

20. "Put [your] abilities to work" (1 Timothy 4:15, TLB).

Chapter 5

1. I've drawn from many sources in telling of this story, including my own research and trips to Oxford. Of great help in putting it all together, however, was David Horan's *Oxford: A Cultural and Literary Companion* (New York: Interlink Books, 2000), 127-30.

2. J. R. R. Tolkien, *The Lord of the Rings, Part 1: The Fellowship of the Ring*, 2d ed. (Boston: Houghton Mifflin, 1965), 283.

3. Tolkien, *The Fellowship of the Ring*, 284.

4. This speech was delivered June 18, 1940. Quoted from Norman Rose, *Churchill: The Unruly Giant* (New York: The Free Press, 1994), 329.

5. Rose, *Churchill*, 2.

6. Cited from Os Guinness, ed., *Unriddling Our Times: Reflections on the Gathering Cultural Crisis* (Grand Rapids, Mich.: Baker Book House, 1999), 114.

7. Adapted from Os Guinness, *Time for Truth* (Grand Rapids, Mich.: Baker, 2000), 21-3.

8. Matthew 5:13-16

9. For additional background on this section of Jesus' teaching, see John R. W. Stott, *Christian Counter-Culture: The Message of the Sermon on the Mount* (Downers Grove, Ill.: InterVarsity, 1978), 57-68.

10. On this, see Malcolm Gladwell, *The Tipping Point: How Little Things Can Make a Big Difference* (Boston: Little, Brown, 2000), 133-68. Gladwell calls this phenomenon the "power of context," and in terms

of epidemics of behavior, he contends that we are sensitive to the conditions and circumstances of the times and places in which they occur.

11. Stott, *Christian Counter-Culture*, 65.

12. The allegory of the cave is contained within Plato's larger conversation on whether universals are real. He expressed his thoughts in two famous passages: "The Divided Line" and "The Allegory of the Cave." On this, see Plato, *The Republic*, trans. F. M. Cornford (Oxford: Oxford University Press, 1941), 213-28.

13. For more on the story of these men, see Elisabeth Elliot, *Through Gates of Splendor* (Wheaton, Ill.: Tyndale, 1981).

14. Matthew 5:13

15. See Stott, *Christian Counter-Culture*, 63.

16. Cassie Bernall's story has been taken, including letters and dialogue, from her mother's book on her life. See Misty Bernall, *She Said Yes* (North Farmington, Pa.: Plough Publishing House, 1999). The comment by Madeleine L'Engle comes from the book's foreword, xiii-iv. Used by permission.

Chapter 6

1. Adapted from Elie Wiesel, *Night*, trans. Stella Rodway (Toronto and New York: Bantam, 1960) 60-2.

2. Adapted from Arnold Burron and Jerry Crews, *Guaranteed Steps to Managing Stress* (Wheaton, Ill.: Tyndale, 1986), 59-60.

3. Job 1:21

4. Job 2:9

5. Job 2:10

6. Job 2:3

7. Julia Sweeney, *God Said, "Ha!"* (New York: Bantam, 1997), 27.

8. See Paul Brand and Philip Yancey, *The Gift of Pain* (Grand Rapids, Mich.: Zondervan, 1997), 3-13.

9. For a discussion of the reason for suffering from a theological point of view, often called theodicy, see James Emery White, *A Search for the Spiritual* (Grand Rapids, Mich.: Baker, 1998).

10. C. S. Lewis, *The Problem of Pain* (New York: Touchstone, 1996), 83.

11. As penned to Sheldon Vanauken and published in Vanauken's *A Severe Mercy* (Toronto: Bantam, 1977), 211.

12. Lewis, *The Problem of Pain*, 85.

13. C. S. Lewis, *A Grief Observed* (San Francisco: Harper & Row, 1961), 32.

14. Aleksandr Solzhenitsyn, *The Gulag Archipelago: 1918–1956, An Experiment in Literary Investigation* (New York: HarperCollins, 1992), 3:615.

15. Adapted from James Dobson, *When God Doesn't Make Sense* (Wheaton, Ill.: Tyndale, 1993), 147.

16. Romans 5:3-4

17. 2 Corinthians 1:3-4, MSG

18. Corrie ten Boom, with John Sherrill and Elizabeth Sherrill, *The Hiding Place* (New York: Bantam, 1971), 217.

19. Adapted from Philip Yancey, *Where Is God When It Hurts?* (Grand Rapids, Mich.: Zondervan, 1977), 88-90.

20. John 9:1-3, MSG

21. 2 Corinthians 12:7-10, TLB

22. Adapted from Charles Stanley, *The Wonderful Spirit-Filled Life* (Nashville, Tenn.: Nelson, 1992), 48-9.

23. Proverbs 3:5

24. C. S. Lewis, *Letters to an American Lady*, ed. Clyde S. Kilby (Grand Rapids, Mich.: Eerdmans, 1967), 114.

25. Yancey, *Where Is God When It Hurts?* 94-5.

Chapter 7

1. Adapted from the foreword to Johann Christoph Arnold, *Why Forgive?* (Farmington, Pa.: Plough Publishing, 2000), ix-x.

2. Adapted from Ravi Zacharias, *Cries of the Heart* (Nashville, Tenn.: Word, 1998), 91-2.

3. Psalm 25:7

4. Isaiah 43:25

5. Jeremiah 31:34

6. Matthew 18:21-22

7. Adapted from Charles Swindoll, *Growing Strong in the Seasons of Life* (Portland, Oreg.: Multnomah, 1983), 286, as well as Leslie B. Flynn, *Great Church Fights* (Wheaton, Ill.: Victor, 1976), 91.

8. Adapted from Alan Loy McGinnis, *The Friendship Factor* (Minneapolis, Minn.: Augsburg, 1979), 156-7. See also Luis Palau, *Experiencing God's Forgiveness: Being Freed from Sin and Guilt* (Portland, Oreg.: Multnomah, 1984), 19.

9. Adapted from Arnold, *Why Forgive?* 59-63.

10. Adapted from David Aikman, *Great Souls: Six Who Changed the Century* (Nashville, Tenn.: Word, 1998), 6.

11. Swindoll, *Growing Strong in the Seasons of Life,* 156.

12. Matthew 7:1-2

13. Matthew 6:14-15

14. Adapted from Ernest Hemingway, "The Capitol of the World," in *The Short Stories of Ernest Hemingway* (New York: Scribner, 1953), 38. See also Philip Yancey's retelling of the tale in *What's So Amazing About Grace?* (Grand Rapids, Mich.: Zondervan, 1997), 38-9. Copyright by Philip D. Yancey. Used by permission of Zondervan Publishing House.

15. Deborah Tannen, *The Argument Culture: Moving from Debate to Dialogue* (New York: Random House, 1998), 3.

16. C. S. Lewis, *Mere Christianity* (New York: Macmillan, 1952), 89.

17. Yancey, *What's So Amazing About Grace?* 84.

18. Anne Lamott, *Traveling Mercies: Some Thoughts on Faith* (New York: Pantheon, 1999), 128.

19. Ephesians 4:32, MSG

20. Colossians 3:13, TLB

21. I've developed and adapted these five steps from the insights and research of David Augsburger, a Christian professor and family therapist who has written a number of excellent books on the subject, including *The Freedom of Forgiveness* (Chicago: Moody, 1988). See particularly pp. 42-4, as well as *Caring Enough to Forgive* (Ventura, Calif.: Regal, 1981).

22. 1 John 4:20-21, MSG

23. Dietrich Bonhoeffer, *Life Together* (New York: Harper & Row, 1954), 36.

24. See Lewis, *Mere Christianity*, 90.

25. John Haggai, *How to Win over Worry*, expanded ed. (Eugene, Oreg.: Harvest House, 1987), 184.

26. Proverbs 19:11

27. C. S. Lewis, *Letters to an American Lady*, ed. Clyde S. Kilby (Grand Rapids, Mich.: Eerdmans, 1967), 107.

28. Lewis, *Letters to an American Lady*, 107.

29. Matthew 5:23-24

30. Matthew 18:15

31. In the case of sexual abuse, particularly if the victim is a minor, this may not be advisable.

32. Helmut Thielicke, *The Waiting Father* (San Francisco: Harper & Row, 1959), 112, as cited in Yancey, *What's So Amazing About Grace?* 91.

33. Larry Crabb, *Inside Out* (Colorado Springs, Colo.: NavPress, 1988), 122.

34. Luke 17:3-4, MSG

35. Adapted from Corrie ten Boom, *Tramp for the Lord* (Old Tappan, N.J.: Revell, 1974), 53-5; also, Corrie ten Boom, with John Sherrill and Elizabeth Sherrill, *The Hiding Place* (New York: Bantam, 1971), 238.

Chapter 8

1. Adapted from the anonymously written article "The War Within: An Anatomy of Lust," *Leadership Journal*, vol. 3, no. 4 (fall 1982): 30-48. Copyright 1982. Reprinted with permission from *Leadership Journal.*

2. James 1:15

3. See Luke 4:1-13.

4. 1 Peter 5:8

5. Gordon MacDonald, *Rebuilding Your Broken World* (Nashville, Tenn.: Oliver Nelson, 1988), 53. It should be noted that MacDonald has been a model of repentance and is fully restored to his wife and family. I share his story only as a result of his own courageous willingness to share publicly the lessons he has learned.

6. Craig Brian Larson, ed., *Illustrations for Preaching and Teaching from Leadership Journal* (Grand Rapids, Mich.: Baker, 1993), 257.

7. 2 Peter 2:14-15

8. Throughout this chapter, sexual temptation is used as something of an ongoing case study. It's not that this is the greatest of temptations—for that, I would nominate pride—but it is the easiest to dissect and occupies a great number of the biblical examples.

9. The word *looks* in Matthew 5:28 is a present tense verb in Greek, indicating that the one who looks in this way makes it a continual habit of life.

10. 1 Corinthians 10:13

11. It should be noted that I am not attempting to make the case that a Christian can ultimately rise above all sin in this life. We can't. Yet we can grow in holiness, maturing in our resistance to temptation and refusing Satan his footholds into our lives that would lead to our spiritual defeat.

12. For the full record of David's moral fall, see 2 Samuel 11.

13. 2 Samuel 11:3

14. J. Allan Petersen, *The Myth of the Greener Grass*, rev. ed. (Wheaton, Ill.: Tyndale, 1991), 23.

15. C. S. Lewis, *The Screwtape Letters*, rev. ed. (New York: Collier, 1982), 30.

16. Dag Hammarskjold, *Markings* (New York: Knopf, 1964), 15.

17. Petersen, *The Myth of the Greener Grass*, 77.

18. Thomas à Kempis, *The Imitation of Christ* (New York: Sheed and Ward, 1950), 31.

19. 2 Timothy 3:16-17, NLT

20. James 4:7, MSG

21. Genesis 39:6-12

22. See 1 Corinthians 6:12-20.

23. The verb is in the present imperative tense.

24. MacDonald, *Rebuilding Your Broken World*, 197.

25. Lamentations 3:40

Chapter 9

1. As quoted by Will Durant and Ariel Durant, *The Lessons of History* (New York: Simon & Schuster, 1968), 53.

2. Adapted from Gordon MacDonald, *The Life God Blesses* (Nashville, Tenn.: Nelson, 1994), 59.

3. 2 Samuel 12:1-10

4. St. John of the Cross, *Dark Night of the Soul,* trans. and ed. E. Allison Peers (Garden City, N.Y.: Image Books, 1959), 59.

5. C. S. Lewis, *The Screwtape Letters*, rev. ed. (New York: Collier, 1982), 61.

6. Jeremiah 8:4-6,9,11-12

7. Søren Kierkegaard, *Purity of Heart Is to Will One Thing*, trans. Douglas V. Steere (New York: Harper Torchbooks, 1956), 186.

8. 2 Corinthians 7:9-10, MSG

9. Kierkegaard, *Purity of Heart Is to Will One Thing,* 44.

10. Albert Camus, *The Fall* (New York: Vintage International, 1991), 81.

11. Psalm 51:1-3

12. Psalm 51:4-6

13. Psalm 51:7-9

14. Psalm 51:10-17

15. Craig Brian Larson, ed., *Illustrations for Preaching and Teaching from Leadership Journal* (Grand Rapids, Mich.: Baker, 1993), 109-10.

16. 1 John 3:19-20, Phillips

17. 1 Peter 1:16, NLT

18. Psalm 32:1-5, MSG

19. Adapted from Verne Becker, Tim Stafford, and Philip Yancey, *What They Never Told Me When I Became a Christian* (Grand Rapids, Mich.: Zondervan, 1991), 52.

20. Taken from Philip D. Yancey, *What's So Amazing About Grace?* (Grand Rapids, Mich.: Zondervan, 1997), 49-52. Used by permission of Zondervan Publishing House.

Chapter 10

1. Adapted from Ken Blanchard, *We Are the Beloved* (Grand Rapids, Mich.: Zondervan, 1994), 7.

2. Andy Seiler, "Arnold's Pumped Up by Career After Last Action-Hero Role," *USA Today,* 24 November 1999, sec. D, p. 4.

3. Anne Lamott, *Traveling Mercies: Some Thoughts on Faith* (New York: Pantheon, 1999), 189.

4. For this idea, see Rabbi Marc Gellman and Monsignor Thomas Hartman, *How Do You Spell God?* (New York: Morrow Junior Books, 1995), 19-24.

5. Mark A. Noll, *The Scandal of the Evangelical Mind* (Grand Rapids, Mich.: Eerdmans, 1994), 3.

6. 1 Corinthians 9:24-27

7. James 2:14

8. James 2:17

9. Matthew 16:24, MSG

10. Matthew 7:23

11. James 2:19, MSG

12. Adapted from Brent Curtis and John Eldredge, *The Sacred Romance* (Nashville, Tenn.: Nelson, 1997), 160.

13. Dialog and excerpts of the song "Do You Love Me" transcribed from the film *Fiddler on the Roof* © 1971 Metro-Goldwyn-Mayer Studios Inc. All rights reserved. Music and lyrics by Sheldon Harnick and Jerry Bock © 1964 (renewed 1992) Mayerling Productions Ltd. and Jerry Bock Enterprises. All rights reserved. Used by permission of Warner Bros. Publications U.S. Inc., Miami, FL 33014.

14. John 1:12

15. This equation first came to my attention through my friend Lee Strobel.

16. 2 Corinthians 5:17, NLT

A Final Word

1. Adapted from an illustration given by Wayne Cordeiro at the Leadership Summit in Chicago, Illinois, August 1999.

2. John 13:3

3. Matthew 19:28-29